The Complete Book of

Arts & Crafts

Edited by Dawn Purney

Design by Betsy E. Snyder

Cover illustration by
Illustrated Alaskan Moose, Inc.

Illustrated by Mary Rojas,
Betsy E. Snyder, Ali Mohrman
and Bot Roda

Table of Contents

Introduction

Dear Parents,

The creative arts are an essential component of childhood development. By using the activities in this book, you will involve your child in experimenting with a variety of techniques to make simple projects. This book is for beginning crafters and young artists. Although the projects are designed for children ages five through nine, many can be adapted for both older and younger children.

Because of the age range of the children using this book, you as the adult need to be sensitive to your child's needs. Most children will need you to read to them. Many children are still developing their fine motor coordination as well. Doing these crafts will give your child good practice. Younger children may need help cutting or may need you to cut out things for them. Do not be concerned if your child needs your help. Do provide your child with extra practice.

Encourage freedom of expression and promote your child's creativity and decision-making skills by allowing for time simply to play and by accepting all final projects as wonderful, which they surely will be!

Many projects offer suggestions after the directions. Feel free to make your own or let your child come up with his/her own variations. Even if the craft "flops," he/she will still have learned something through the process of making it. You can always go back together and try the craft again.

As with most instructive books, make sure to read all the directions before starting a project. The materials list will sometimes give you a choice. The directions refer to the first item listed but will work with whichever material you chose.

Many of these projects can—and should—be displayed. Seeing that his/her own handiwork is good enough to be hung up in your home helps your child develop a sense of pride and self-worth. Some projects can be used for school projects. Your child can also give away his or her projects as gifts. The crafts in the Useful Crafts and Holiday and Toy sections are especially good to give as gifts.

You will probably be looking at several things when choosing a craft, such as what materials are needed or how long it will take to make. The index in the back lists each craft and key factors that can help you find just the right projects for your child.

Most importantly, have fun making crafts!

Sincerely,
American Education Publishing

Using This Book

- After choosing a craft, check the list marked "What you'll need." These items are the art supplies and tools you will need to make the craft. Some materials are listed as "optional." That means that you can use them, but you do not need them for the craft. You might base your decision on whether you want a certain look or whether that item is readily available.

- The next thing you should do is read all the directions before you start the craft. You should also read the "Suggestion(s)," which might involve different tools or materials.

- Then, collect the materials and follow "Here's how" to make the craft.

Improving Cutting Skills

Some children who are still learning how to use scissors cannot seem to cut on the lines no matter how hard they try. This problem can often be fixed in a fun way. Check to see "who is in the driver's seat"; that is, check for correct finger placement. Correct finger placement involves the use of the thumb and the middle finger, not the index finger. The middle finger has more strength and maintains better control.

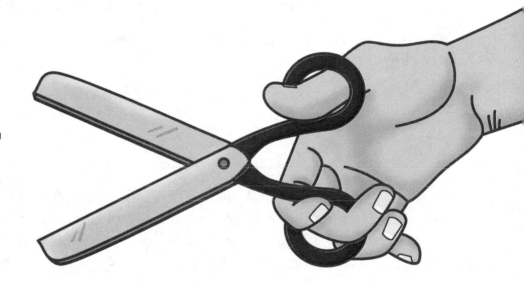

If the opening in the handle is large enough, both the index and middle fingers can be inserted. However, the index finger is only "going along for the ride." The thumb and the middle finger do all the work (driving).

If your child's fingers are too large for the scissors, he/she may need to readjust the grip and eliminate the use of the index finger when cutting.

Be ready to do any cutting for your child as needed. A younger child especially may need supervision. Don't let him/her get discouraged if you need to take over. Continue to provide your child with opportunities to practice cutting.

Painting Tips

Watercolor paints, the kind in a plastic, boxed palette, are used most often in this book. When tempera paint is used, you will find liquid tempera more convenient and easier to measure than the powdered form.

Some activities call for paint dishes. Pie pans or foam trays work well for these activities. However, it is recommended that you use clean foam trays from supermarket-packaged baked goods, fruits or vegetables, because meat and poultry trays are difficult to disinfect. You can also mix paint in an ice cube tray or muffin tin.

Brush Care

- Dip just the tip of the brush in the water and in the paint.

- Use a different brush, or at least rinse your brush thoroughly, when changing colors.

- When using the same color, there is no need to dip the brush in water after every stroke.

- Do not twist or pull on the hairs of the brush—they might fall out.

Paint Care

Of all the art mediums that children enjoy using, watercolor paints seem to be a favorite. Teach your child to keep the crispness in paint colors by treating the set properly. Have your child always use the brushes and paints correctly and always go through a standard clean-up routine at the end of each project.

If your set of paints is already muddied, have your child clean them using the following steps:

1. Beginning with the lightest colors, place a few drops of water in each tray to soften the paint.

2. Rinse the brush.

3. Gently blot the brush dry on a paper towel.

4. Use the dry brush as a "mop." Soak up the dirty water, and with it will come the dirty paint.

Exploring Colors

Every beginning artist should experience making his/her own colors. Mixing colors is a fun and memorable process—as well as educational. An easy way to do this is to allow your child to explore the relationships among colors by mixing paints on his/her own. With an older child, use the terms primary, secondary and complementary colors.

Have your child work with small amounts of primary tempera paints (red, yellow and blue). The secondary colors can be produced by mixing small, equal amounts of paint colors on a foam tray. (Be sure to clean the brush before mixing other colors.)

Examples:

Mix Primary Colors	Produce Secondary Color	
Red and Yellow	Orange	
Red and Blue	Purple	
Blue and Yellow	Green	

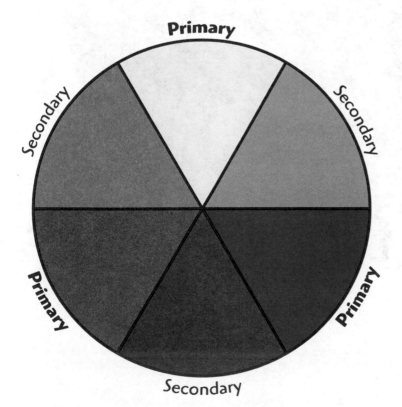

Identify complementary colors by finding which colors lie directly opposite each other on the color wheel. Complementary colors look good together. They can also be used to produce other colors. If equal amounts of complementary colors are mixed together, brown is produced.

The Color Wheel

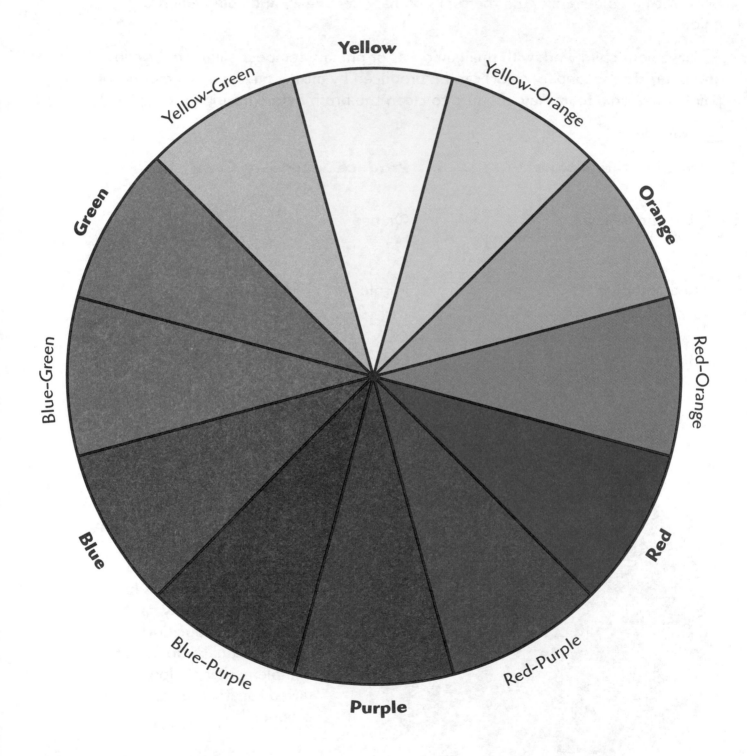

Yellow

Yellow-Green

Yellow-Orange

Green

Orange

Blue-Green

Red-Orange

Blue

Red

Blue-Purple

Red-Purple

Purple

Paper Creations

Paper art can be simple, fun and very creative. You can tear it, cut it, draw on it, paint it, layer it, color it, crumple it, fold it or add it to another material. Paper is used to create many forms of art, such as drawing, painting, paper maché and origami. For example, by using simple folding techniques, you can turn a plain sheet of paper into a three-dimensional sailboat or even a spring flower.

The Paper Creations section uses a variety of paper products and things such as crayons, scissors and glue. After you turn your simple paper into a rabbit or a beautiful butterfly, you may never look at a sheet of paper the same way again!

Origami Sailboat

Origami is the ancient art of folding paper. Amazing figures can be made without cutting or gluing!

What you'll need

☐ white construction paper or any unlined paper
☐ crayons or markers
☐ scissors

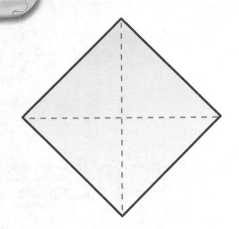

1. Cut the construction paper into a square with 4-inch sides.

2. Fold your paper in half diagonally, then fold it in half diagonally again.

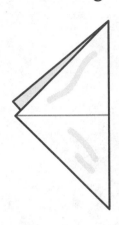

3. Unfold the paper once to make a triangle.

4. Fold one edge up to meet the halfway line (see diagram on the right).

5. Fold the bottom corners on the boat back behind, as shown. Tuck them in together to keep them in place.

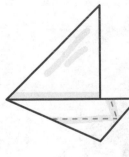

6. Decorate your sail with crayons or markers, and write the boat's name on one side.

Boy Oh Buoy

Snow People Paper Dolls

Make an entire family of snow people just by folding and cutting! Use colored paper, markers and glitter to decorate them.

What you'll need

- [ ] rectangular white paper (18" x 24" works best)
- [ ] markers or crayons
- [ ] pencil
- [ ] scissors
- [ ] glue (optional)
- [ ] scraps of colored construction paper (optional)

Here's how . . .

1. Make an accordion fold with the white paper as shown. When folded, the width of the paper should be about 3 or 4 inches across. (The number of folds depends on your paper size.)

2. Use a pencil to draw a snow person outline that goes a little bit off the paper, as shown. You may want an adult to draw it for you.

3. Cut out the snow person, cutting through all the layers of paper at once. Do not cut off the entire fold.

4. Unfold your paper and draw clothes and faces for each figure. Cut out hat and scarf shapes from the colored construction paper and glue them onto the snow people.

Suggestion

● You can create other figures, such as angels or children holding hands.

Woven Place Mats

Weaving your own place mats is easy and fun—and they make mealtime special for your family!

What you'll need

- [ ] 12" x 18" construction paper in 2 different-colored sheets
- [ ] ruler
- [ ] pencil
- [ ] scissors
- [ ] glue

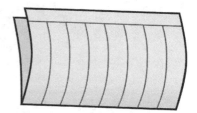

1. Take one sheet of construction paper and draw a line 1 inch from the top. Fold the construction paper in half, as shown.

2. Draw lines about 1 1/2 inches apart from the top line to the fold, as shown.

3. Cut on the lines from the fold to the line.

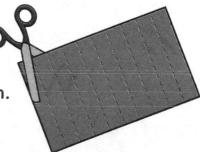

4. Cut the second piece of construction paper into 1 1/2 inch strips across the width of the paper, as shown.

5. Use these strips to weave through the strips of the first sheet of construction paper. To weave means to take the strip under the paper, then take it over the paper at the next opening.

6. When you have finished weaving the entire mat, glue the ends of the strips down on the back side.

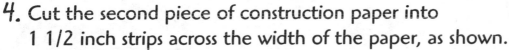

Suggestion

● Draw and cut wavy instead of straight lines (steps 2 and 3) for a more fun look.

Spring Flowers

Brighten someone's day! Make several flowers for a paper bouquet.

What you'll need

- [ ] construction paper, green and other colors
- [ ] crayons or markers
- [ ] scissors
- [ ] glue
- [ ] paper hole punch (optional)

1. Cut a circle about 1 1/2 inches across out of construction paper.

2. Glue dots from a hole punch or color a design in the center of the flower.

3. Cut out 1/2 inch by 2 1/2 inch strips of construction paper to make petals.

4. Glue the ends of the petals together, as shown.

5. Glue the petals onto the back of the circle, as shown. You may need to hold it for a minute while it dries.

6. Cut a stem and some leaves from the green construction paper and glue them to the flower.

Suggestions

● Glue another ring of petals behind the first set.

● Use longer strips to make longer petals.

● See page 170 for directions on making a vase for these flowers.

Cardboard Caterpillar

You can make wild and wacky or simple and sweet caterpillars using household materials and a little imagination.

What you'll need

- ❏ paper towel or toilet paper cardboard rolls
- ❏ colorful paper of any and all types (tissue paper, wrapping paper, construction paper)
- ❏ pipe cleaner
- ❏ pom-poms, buttons or cotton balls
- ❏ wiggly eyes
- ❏ glue
- ❏ scissors
- ❏ paper hole punch

1. Cut a strip of paper 1 inch wide. Wrap it around the cardboard roll. Trim off any extra paper.

2. Cut more strips in different colors the same length, using the first strip as your pattern.

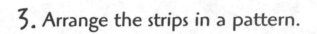

3. Arrange the strips in a pattern.

4. Glue each strip around the cardboard roll.

5. Punch a hole close to one end of the roll. Bend a pipe cleaner in half and stick the middle in the hole. The parts sticking out form the antennae.

6. Place a pom-pom sticking out of the same end.

7. Glue wiggly eyes on the pom-pom.

Suggestion

- Use other small decorations to create your own Cardboard Creature.

Autumn Tree

Make your own fall tree as brilliant and full as you like, simply by using colorful paper, a pencil and some glue.

What you'll need

- ☐ light blue and brown construction paper
- ☐ tissue paper, in fall leaf colors
- ☐ pencil with an eraser
- ☐ crayons
- ☐ glue
- ☐ scissors

Here's how . . .

1. Using brown construction paper, tear one or more tree trunk shapes. This gives a more natural look to the tree.

2. Glue your tree trunks to the light blue construction paper. To make your design more interesting, tear tree limb shapes and add them to your trees.

3. Color in the ground around the trees.

4. Cut 1-inch squares of tissue paper to make the leaves.

5. Wrap each square around a pencil eraser, dip it in glue and press it in place on your tree.

6. Add different colored leaves to your trees until they are as full as you like.

Suggestion

● Use green and red or pink tissue paper to make a flowering tree in spring.

"Stained Glass" Butterfly

Look! Is that a butterfly in your house? Your friends will think so when they see your colorful see-through butterfly!

What you'll need

- 12" x 18" black construction paper
- tissue paper in assorted colors
- pencil
- scissors
- glue
- string or yarn
- paper hole punch

Here's how . . .

1. Fold the black paper in half lengthwise.

2. Draw half an outline of a butterfly.

3. Repeat the outline 1 inch inside the first outline, as shown. Leave space between the outlines.

4. With the design still folded in half, cut out the outline and inside of the shapes. Leave the borders uncut.

5. Unfold the butterfly and cut tissue paper to cover each opening. Make the tissue paper slightly larger than the opening.

6. Glue the tissue paper to the back of the butterfly covering each opening.

7. Punch a hole near the top and tie on a string.

8. Hang the butterfly from the ceiling or in a window.

Suggestions

- Try your own wing design.

- If you hang your butterfly, you may want to glue another black construction paper frame onto the back so it looks nice from both sides.

Reflecting Pool

Use this easy trick to make a masterpiece. One turn of your paper and you've created a beautiful reflecting pool!

What you'll need

- ☐ white paper
- ☐ pencil
- ☐ crayons
- ☐ watercolor or watered-down tempera paint
- ☐ paintbrush

Here's how . . .

1. Use a pencil to draw a horizon line separating the sky from the water across your paper.

2. Draw scenery above your horizon line. Possible choices include mountains, sun, land, trees or boats.

3. Turn the paper upside down.

4. Repeat the drawing to create the reflection, using wavy lines across the paper to imitate the movement of the water.

5. Turn the drawing to its first position.

6. With crayons, color the parts identically that are above and below the horizon line.

7. Paint over the entire surface below the horizon line with a coat of blue paint. Use wavy strokes for water movement.

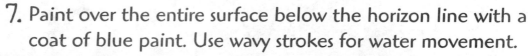

Sunshine Ornament

Use pieces of crayon to make . . . a window ornament? You won't believe how bright it will look.

What you'll need

- [ ] two 9" paper plates
- [ ] crayons in shades of yellow, red and orange
- [ ] wax paper
- [ ] yellow, red or orange construction paper
- [ ] an iron and ironing board
- [ ] paper towels
- [ ] cheese or vegetable grater
- [ ] yarn, string or thread for hanging
- [ ] white glue
- [ ] scissors
- [ ] pencil
- [ ] an adult

Here's how . . .

1. Carefully cut out the centers from the paper plates, leaving the rims uncut.

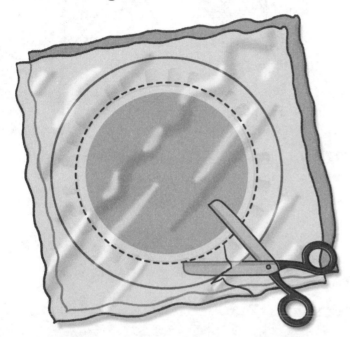

2. Cut 2 sheets of wax paper slightly larger than the hole in the plate.

3. Draw and cut out a circle from the construction paper. Make it smaller than a soda pop can. This is the middle of your sun.

4. Protect your ironing board with several layers of paper towels. Place one wax paper circle on the towels and place your cut out construction paper drawing on top of the wax paper.

5. Remove the labels from your crayons. Have an adult use a grater to shave small chips off each crayon so they fall around the paper cut out. You need only a few chips of each color. These will become the sun's rays.

(continued on next page)

6. Carefully cover the picture with the other wax paper circle. Add another layer of paper towels on top of the wax paper.

7. Have an adult press the two wax paper circles together with a warm iron until the crayon chips are melted.

8. Apply glue around the inside rim of one plate and place your pressed wax paper picture inside the glued rim.

9. Place one end of a long piece of yarn above the picture to be the hanger.

10. Place the other plate rim inside the glued rim containing the picture ornament. Make sure the yarn is between the plates.

11. When the glue is dry, hang your ornament in a window.

Suggestion

● Create these other variations below or make up your own!

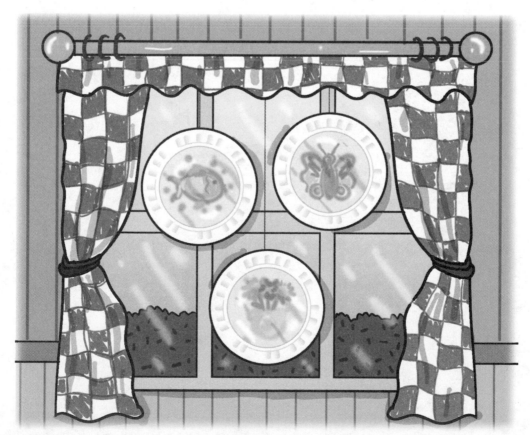

Stencils

Cut stencils in the shapes of letters, numbers, patterns or symbols. Fill them in with crayons, markers or paint to create cards, make patterns or just to practice writing.

Here's how . . .

1. Draw shapes, numbers or letters with a pen on the plastic lids.

2. Have an adult use sharp scissors to poke through each lid within the design and begin cutting out the shape.

3. Finish cutting out the shape or have an adult cut it out for you.

4. Trace the shapes onto white paper.

What you'll need

- ☐ plastic lids from coffee cans or margarine containers
- ☐ white paper
- ☐ scissors
- ☐ pencil
- ☐ pen
- ☐ an adult

Painting Projects

If you can pick up a brush, you can be a painter! Since the beginning of time, people have been using brushes and other objects to swirl colored dyes and paints around in order to communicate and be creative. The first "masterpieces" may have been painted on the walls of ancient caves!

This section shows you how to use "brush substitutes" like cotton swabs, rags and even marbles! The first painters used natural dyes and berries to create their own paint. You can create your own paint, too, using common items from around the house. Don't forget to prepare your work area before you begin. That means covering the work surface with newspaper; using an old paint shirt to protect your clothes; and having plenty of soap, water and paper towels on hand for cleanup.

For more painting tips, turn to page 6.

Beyond the Brush

Who says you need a paintbrush to paint? Experiment with these other kinds of "paintbrushes" or come up with some different ones of your own!

Paint With:

Cotton Swabs

You can use swabs to "draw" with the paint, making more detailed pictures than those painted with most kinds of brushes.

Feathers

One way to use feathers is to paint them with a paintbrush, then paint with the feather as a brush while it is still wet.

Rag Painting

Tear a cotton rag into a 2"x 8" strip and knot it in the middle. Hold the knotted piece of cotton rag by both ends. Coat the knot by rolling it in tempera paint. Roll the rag across the paper, making uneven tracks with the paint-soaked knot.

Toy Cars

Dip a toy car in paint to coat the wheels. Then, drive it over the paper to make roads and tracks. When the painting dries, cut out pictures of cars and trucks from toy catalogs or magazines and glue them onto the "road map."

Sponges

Sponges give a very different texture. A kitchen sponge can be used "as is" or cut into a shape to use as a stencil.

Water

A warm, sunny day can inspire you to create designs with water on pavement. Recycle squeeze-type dishwashing liquid bottles for squirting lines and letters on pavement. You can also use wide brushes and sponges.

Marble Painting

You never know what kind of design you'll get when you use marbles to create this project! Roll the marbles, and watch the design appear!

What you'll need

- [ ] marbles or small rubber balls
- [ ] pie pan or another type of metal pan
- [ ] tempera paints
- [ ] white paper
- [ ] scissors

Here's how . . .

1. Cut paper to fit in the bottom of a pie pan.

2. Squeeze a few drops of paint onto the paper. Then, put a few marbles into the pan. You can use different colors of paint at once or wait until one color dries before adding another color.

3. Hold the pan and gently roll the marbles back and forth through the paint.

Dip 'n' Dye Designs

Watch the colors flow and change on their own! Experiment to create colorful patterns.

What you'll need

- ☐ flattened coffee filters or paper towels
- ☐ food coloring
- ☐ empty margarine tubs or muffin tins
- ☐ water
- ☐ toothpicks
- ☐ scissors (optional)

Here's how . . .

1. Fill the tubs with water. Add a few drops of food coloring to each one. Mix each with a toothpick.

2. Fold your coffee filter in half several times.

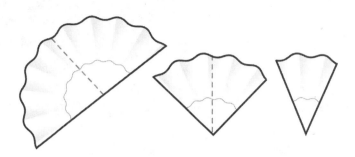

3. If you want, cut out patterns on the edges. Be careful not to cut off the entire edge.

4. Dip each corner into a different color. The color will spread and run into the other colors. You may see that two colors mixed together make a new color.

5. Unfold the filter to dry.

Suggestions

- Instead of dipping the coffee filter, unfold the filter and paint it with watercolors.

- Cut the dried designs into flower shapes. Add green construction paper stems and leaves.

Eyedropper Art

What a weird brush! The dropper lets you choose where you want each color to be.

What you'll need

- [ ] eyedropper
- [ ] food coloring
- [ ] paper towels or flattened coffee filters
- [ ] construction paper
- [ ] muffin tin, ice-cube tray, foam cups or egg carton
- [ ] toothpicks
- [ ] water
- [ ] glue

Here's how . . .

1. Fill a tin with water and add a few drops of food coloring to each section. Mix each with a toothpick.

2. Squeeze the rubber end of the eyedropper and dip the other end into a color. Stop squeezing to let the paint fill the dropper.

3. Squeeze the eyedropper to put drops of color on a paper towel.

4. When the paper towel is dry, frame it with construction or mount it on a sheet of black construction paper.

Suggestion

- When your design is dry, make a butterfly. Gather the paper towel together in the middle and loop a colorful pipe cleaner around it for the body. Then, twist the pipe cleaner to form antennae.

Printing With Paint

Printmaking gives you a way to make a design over and over. There are lots of ways to make prints using paper, blocks and even leaves!

Paint, Fold, Print!

Fold your paper in half. Then, open it up and paint only on one side of the fold. Fold your paper again and press down on it. When you open the paper, both sides will be printed with the same image.

Alphabet Block Prints

Using wood alphabet blocks with raised letters, dip each block into a pie pan filled with tempera paint. Press the block onto construction paper, then lift it off, straight up. Spell your word in reverse order. Then, hold your paper up to a mirror to decode!

Object Printing

Use any small objects, such as combs, glasses, jar lids, containers, cookie cutters, etc. Dip objects, one at a time, into tempera paint. Press the object onto construction paper, then lift it off, straight up.

Leaf Printing

With the leaf on a baking pan or foam tray, apply an even coat of paint onto the vein-side of the leaf. Paint may be applied with a roller or with brushes. Place a sheet of paper on top of the painted side of the leaf and rub gently with your fingers. Remove the paper and allow time for the paint to dry.

Suggestion

- When done on large paper, any of these prints can be used as wrapping paper.

Vegetable & Fruit Prints

Good food makes great pictures! Let an adult help you do the cutting.

What you'll need

- ☐ vegetable or fruit pieces (onions, cabbage, apples, star fruit, mushrooms, etc.)
- ☐ tempera paint
- ☐ pie pans or aluminum foil
- ☐ paper
- ☐ knife (for the adult to use)
- ☐ butter knife or pencil (optional)
- ☐ an adult

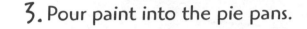

Here's how . . .

1. Have an adult cut each vegetable in half.

2. If desired, use the butter knife to carve out a large outline or picture on the vegetable. Keep it simple.

3. Pour paint into the pie pans.

4. Dip the vegetable or fruit half in the paint. Blot it on scrap paper to even out the paint.

5. Stamp the vegetable half onto the paper gently. Then, lift it straight up.

6. Dip and stamp again to create a design.

7. Continue to stamp, experimenting with placing your stamp in different directions and creating overlapping shapes.

Suggestion

● Have an adult cut the vegetable into different shapes instead of in half.

Roll That Print

Make your own designer paint roller—perfect for making borders or entire pictures!

What you'll need

- [ ] small, sturdy cardboard rolls
- [ ] yarn
- [ ] tempera paint
- [ ] paintbrushes
- [ ] dishes for paint and glue
- [ ] white glue
- [ ] paper
- [ ] scissors

Here's how . . .

1. Cut pieces of yarn 1 to 12 inches long. Then, dip the yarn into a dish of glue.

2. Attach the yarn to the cardboard rolls in patterns, and let it dry thoroughly.

3. Once dry, use a paintbrush to paint the yarn.

4. Roll the painted roll on paper to make print designs.

Suggestion

● This makes a perfect border for other art projects.

by Matthew

Block Prints

Use block prints to make holiday cards or birthday party invitations.

What you'll need

- [ ] paintbrushes, including one with a small rounded end
- [ ] construction paper
- [ ] foam tray
- [ ] tempera paints
- [ ] paint dishes
- [ ] paint dishes
- [ ] scissors
- [ ] pencil (optional)

Here's how . . .

1. Trim off the curved edges on the foam tray to make a flat surface.

2. Paint the foam evenly with a paintbrush.

3. Place your paper over the foam block and press it down smoothly and firmly. *(continued on next page)*

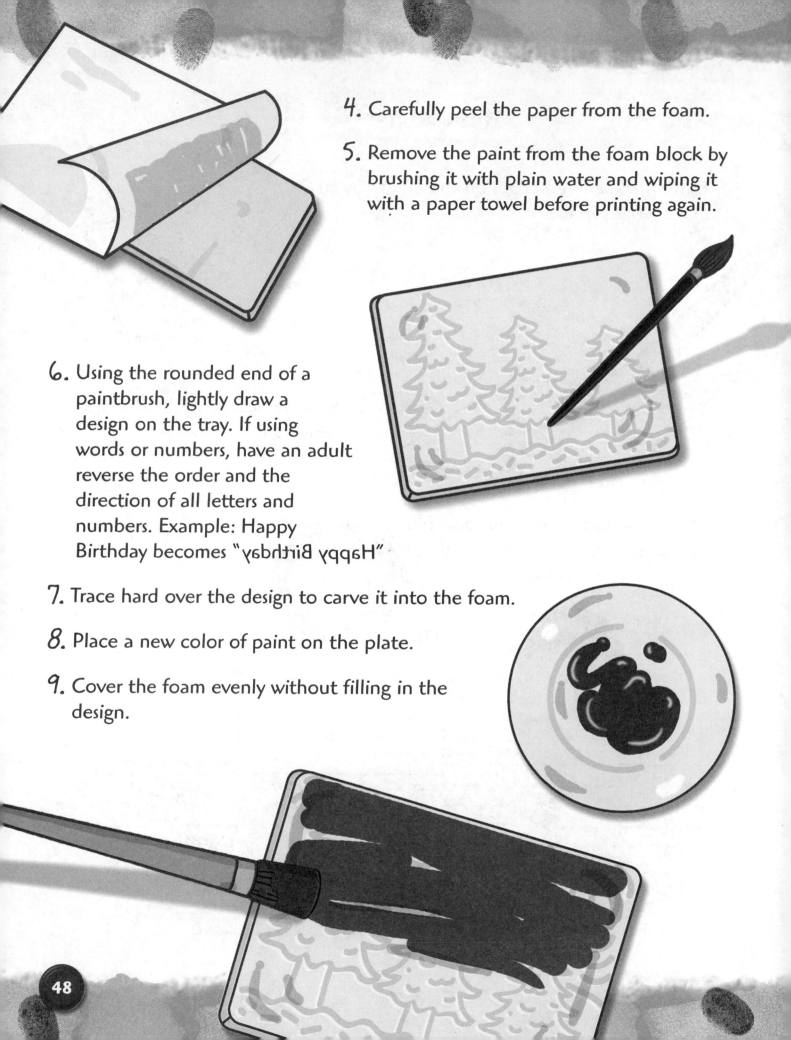

4. Carefully peel the paper from the foam.

5. Remove the paint from the foam block by brushing it with plain water and wiping it with a paper towel before printing again.

6. Using the rounded end of a paintbrush, lightly draw a design on the tray. If using words or numbers, have an adult reverse the order and the direction of all letters and numbers. Example: Happy Birthday becomes "ʎɐpɥʇɹᴉᗺ ʎddɐH"

7. Trace hard over the design to carve it into the foam.

8. Place a new color of paint on the plate.

9. Cover the foam evenly without filling in the design.

10. Place the foam block you carved directly over the solid block print and press the foam down right on top of the paper.

11. If the print is not dark enough, press the block down again, even more firmly.

12. Carefully peel the paper from the foam.

13. Clean the foam block before printing again.

Suggestions

● Get the foam trays from grocery stores. Many stores will even donate them. Ask for **unused** trays at the meat or produce departments.

● Use ink and a brayer (an ink roller) instead of paint and paintbrushes.

paint

pail

paint

Leaf Designs

Collect your favorite kinds of leaves. Then, follow the instructions to make your own woods picture.

What you'll need

- [ ] fresh leaves, various shapes and sizes
- [ ] watercolor paints in fall leaf colors
- [ ] paintbrushes
- [ ] pencil
- [ ] black crayon
- [ ] white construction paper

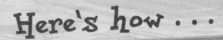

Here's how . . .

1. With your pencil, trace the outlines of leaves onto white construction paper. Make sure to fill the entire page.

2. Trace over each leaf shape with a thick line of black crayon.

3. Paint the inside of each leaf shape with different fall colors. The black crayon outline will keep the colors from running together.

Suggestions

- Use different color crayons for the leaf outlines.

- Paint the white background area.

Starry Night Scene

This project sparkles even more with fluorescent or glitter crayons!

What you'll need

- ☐ watercolor paint
- ☐ paintbrush (a flat 1" brush works best)
- ☐ crayons
- ☐ white construction paper
- ☐ poster board or heavy paper
- ☐ scissors

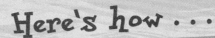

Here's how . . .

1. Draw and cut out several star shapes from the poster board to use as stencils or patterns to trace.

2. Use crayons to trace your stars and draw a night sky design on the paper. Make sure to draw enough stars to fill the entire page. Color heavily.

3. Use dark blue or black watercolors to paint over the entire paper. Paint over your design only one time.

Suggestion

● Add planets, moons, shooting stars, spaceships or anything else you can think of to your Starry Night.

Snowy Painting

Your snowy scene looks almost real with this project. Create another background scene for a completely different picture!

What you'll need

- [ ] dark blue or black construction paper
- [ ] construction paper in other colors
- [ ] thick white tempera paint
- [ ] small sponge
- [ ] cotton balls
- [ ] pie pan
- [ ] aluminum foil
- [ ] glue
- [ ] scissors

1. Cut colored construction paper into various sizes of triangles, squares and rectangles. Use them to create a nighttime city scene of buildings and houses on black or dark blue construction paper.

2. When you are satisfied with your scene, glue the paper shapes in place.

3. Cut out window shapes from aluminum foil, and glue them to the buildings.

4. Pour a small amount of white tempera paint into a pie pan.

5. Dip a sponge into the paint, then blot the paint gently onto the paper to create snow.

6. Stretch cotton balls across the bottom of the paper to make more snow. Glue them in place.

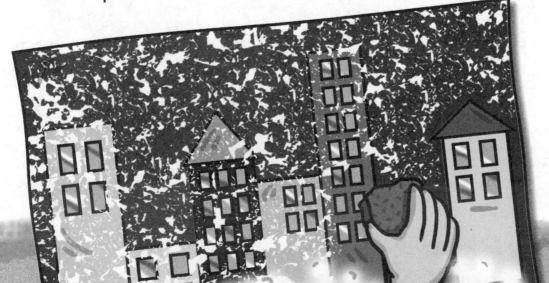

Fun With Fingerpaints

Which is more fun—making the picture or looking at it when it's done? With fingerpaints, it's both! Large, glossy fingerpainting paper is best, but you can use other paper or even another smooth, easy-to-clean surface. Here are several different recipes for you to make your own set of paints. With each set, use your fingers to draw and to add texture to your picture.

Flour and Salt Fingerpaint

This fingerpaint has a grainy quality, providing a different sensory experience. Combine 1 cup flour with 1 1/2 teaspoons of salt (or sand). Add 1 cup of water. Food coloring is optional.

Pudding Prints

Fingerpaint using pudding. Then, carefully lay a sheet of paper over your picture, press lightly and peel back the paper slowly for a copy.

Laundry Detergent Fingerpaint

This type of fingerpaint may be used on a smooth tabletop or on fingerpaint paper. Beat detergent into a small amount of water until you have the consistency of whipped cream. If you are using paper, you can add tempera paint or food coloring and mix it well. Make sure to keep your hands away from your eyes while using this paint.

Textured Fingerpaint

Mix one of the following ingredients into the paint you made: sawdust, coffee grounds, uncooked rice or flour. To make super slippery paint, add dishwashing liquid or glycerin. For sticky paint that dries with a glossy finish, add corn syrup.

Shaving Cream Fingerpaint

Only a small amount of shaving cream is needed to paint on a non-wood tabletop. It actually cleans the table as you work with it. Since the end product cannot be saved, consider taking photos of the artist at work.

Puffy Paint Pictures

Follow this recipe, and you'll have three-dimensional paint! Wait until it's dry—it's as much fun to touch as it is to see.

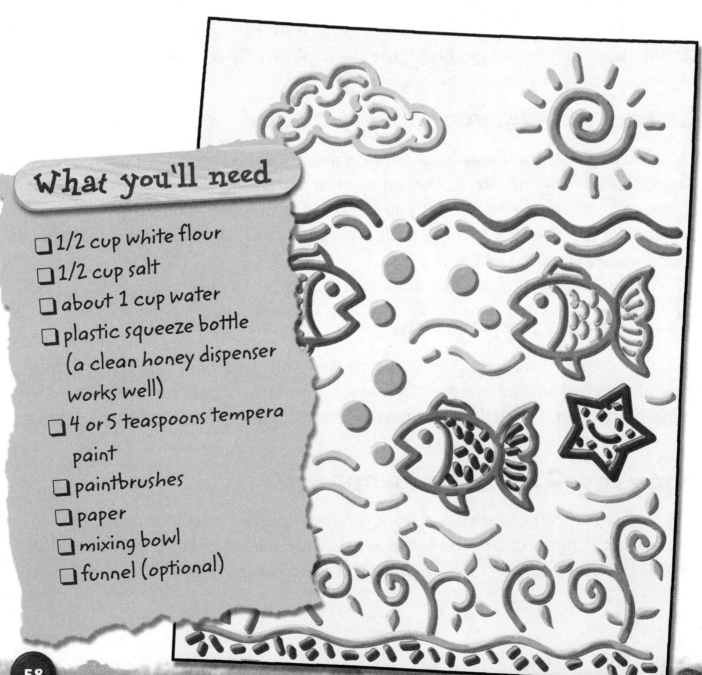

What you'll need

- ☐ 1/2 cup white flour
- ☐ 1/2 cup salt
- ☐ about 1 cup water
- ☐ plastic squeeze bottle (a clean honey dispenser works well)
- ☐ 4 or 5 teaspoons tempera paint
- ☐ paintbrushes
- ☐ paper
- ☐ mixing bowl
- ☐ funnel (optional)

1. Stir together the flour, salt and about half the water in the bowl.

2. Add the tempera paint.

3. Slowly add more water until the mixture can be poured but is not runny.

4. Use the funnel to pour the mixture into a squeeze bottle.

5. Squeeze the paint onto paper. Let the picture dry for several hours.

Suggestion

● Use puffy paint and index cards to make a set of "touchy-feely alphabet cards." They make learning letters fun! You could even use them for a game by putting the letters in a grocery bag and identifying each letter by touch ("This feels like the letter B").

Tie Dyeing

Decorate your own clothes with this special project—with your parent's permission!

What you'll need

- ☐ a piece of cotton clothing—a tee shirt works well*
- ☐ fabric dye**
- ☐ buckets or other containers for dye, 1 for each color
- ☐ large plastic bag or piece of plastic
- ☐ rubber gloves
- ☐ rubber bands (optional)
- ☐ eyedropper, squeeze bottle or paintbrush (optional)
- ☐ an adult

* Have an adult wash the piece of clothing before doing this project. Do not use fabric softeners or dryer sheets.

** Any kind will do, but make sure to read the label before buying it, some dyes call for extra ingredients.

Here's how . . .

1. Have an adult make the dye, following the directions on the package. Anyone working with the dye throughout the project should wear rubber gloves. Doing the project outside is ideal.

2. Tie off the tee shirt. You can knot sections or bundle up sections and put rubber bands on them. See page 62 for different ways to tie it off. Whichever way you choose, make sure to do it tightly, so that dye stays out of those areas.

3. Have an adult dye your shirt. See page 63 for different ways to dye it. Whichever way you choose, remember that the longer you leave the fabric in the dye, the darker the color will be. Also, the dye will be lighter when dry. To mix colors on your shirt, dye it with a new color. If you want the colors to be more separate, let them dry first.

4. Dry the fabric completely on plastic for 1–3 days.

5. Rinse your project in warm water, one section at a time, then in cool water. Take off the rubber bands (or untie the knots) and rinse the shirt again.

6. Have an adult wash the shirt alone before adding it to the regular laundry.

Suggestions

● Some dyes will set better if you have an adult place the fabric between two sheets of paper and steam it with an iron.

● Tie dye scarves, socks, hats, pillowcases, fabric napkins—anything made with cotton fabric.

Ways to Wrap the Shirt:

Each shirt is its own original project. Each one will be different even if you wrap it the same way!

Regular Tie Dye: ▶
Tie knots in sections of the fabric all over the shirt. Dip different sections into the dye, switching colors as you choose.

◀Sunburst:
Pinch the fabric near the center of the shirt. Lift up and twist it into a tight spiral. Then, roll it into the shape of a donut. Keep it in place with rubber bands. Drip dye on the top, then turn it over and drip dye on top again or dip it into one color.

Star: ▶
Choose five places on the shirt to be the points of your star. Bring the edges of them to the center of the shirt. Put rubber bands around the rest of the "arms." Dye the center using a squeeze bottle or eye dropper. Use a different color on the next sections out from the center. Change colors when you get to the second set of sections from the center, and so on.

Ways to Dye the Shirt:

- Dunk the entire shirt in one color. If you want to change the color, dunk it in another color afterwards.

- Dip sections into a color. Dip sections into different colors if desired. The colors will probably run together depending on how close they are.

- Use an eyedropper or a squeeze bottle to make designs and to keep the colors more separated.

Sunset Silhouette

A silhouette is a dark shadow against a lighter background. This picture looks just like what you really see at sunset!

What you'll need

- ☐ watercolor paints
- ☐ black tempera paint or black construction paper
- ☐ paintbrush
- ☐ white paper
- ☐ glue
- ☐ scissors (if construction paper is used)

Here's how . . .

1. Dampen the entire surface of the white paper using a paintbrush and water.

2. Using sunset colors from the watercolor paints such as red and orange, paint one strip at a time across your paper as shown. Because the paper is wet, the colors will run together.

3. Let the paint dry completely.

4. Make silhouette figures and scenery by painting with black tempera paint or cutting out a scene from the black construction paper. Do not worry about small details, they do not show.

Suggestions

● Experiment with red and blue watercolors to produce purple, and create sunrise background scenes.

● Try this craft on watercolor paper.

Blob-Print Kite

Look! This kite flies on your wall as a beautiful *inside* decoration!

What you'll need

- 9" square white construction paper
- tempera paint (make sure it's thick)
- paintbrushes
- crayons or markers
- yarn
- tissue paper
- tape or glue
- paper hole punch or scissors
- stapler

1. Fold the construction paper square in half diagonally, then unfold it.

2. Paint or drop blobs of different-colored paint on one side of the paper.

3. Refold the paper down the center and press the paper halves together.

4. Unfold it, then let your print dry.

5. Use crayons or markers to draw a border around your kite.

6. Punch a hole at the bottom of the kite, and use the yarn to add a tail.

7. Make bows with tissue paper and yarn, as shown.

8. Tie the bows onto the kite tail, and cut off the extra yarn.

A Mixed Bag of Colors

Try this fun—and non-messy—activity to experiment with mixing your colors!

What you'll need

- ☐ tempera paint
- ☐ 1 cup of powdered laundry detergent
- ☐ resealable plastic bags
- ☐ food coloring
- ☐ mixing bowls
- ☐ water
- ☐ spoon

Here's how . . .

1. Place the laundry detergent in a mixing bowl and add water slowly, while stirring. The mixture should remain thick.

2. Divide the mixture into separate bowls and add a different color to each one.

3. Spoon a small amount of two colors into a plastic bag and seal the bag.

4. Gently rub the soapy mixture together and make the two colors blend together to become a third color.

5. Use a different plastic bag for each color combination you make.

Music Makers

Have you ever heard a marching band? Or a symphony? How about someone humming a tune? Well, those are all examples of music, and they are also examples of art.

This section has some great music and instrument-making projects. Use the finished instruments to play as you listen to music. Get some friends together and make your own band! Or make up your own music as you go along.

The instruments in this section are made to be shaken, strummed and tapped. You can even hum or blow into some of the instruments to make different kinds of sounds! You can make kazoos, drums, tambourines, shakers and more. You don't have to follow the instructions exactly—use your imagination and make your own variations. Who knows? You may invent an instrument that you can name after yourself!

Homemade Kazoo

If you can hum, you can already play this easy-to-make instrument! Make a kazoo for a friend, and you can play a duet together.

What you'll need

- ☐ cardboard roll
- ☐ wax paper
- ☐ rubber bands
- ☐ crayons, markers, stickers or paint
- ☐ paper hole punch or scissors
- ☐ an adult

Here's how . . .

1. Decorate the cardboard roll using crayons.

2. Have an adult punch out or poke several holes in one end of the roll.

3. Cover that end and the holes with wax paper held on tightly with a rubber band.

4. Hum into the open end of the roll with fingers placed lightly on the wax paper. Put your finger over one or several holes. Experiment with covering and uncovering the holes as you hum.

Suggestion

● Use a comb instead of the cardboard roll. Loosely wrap the wax paper around the comb. Fasten it on with a rubber band. Hold the comb to your lips and hum!

Kid-Size Drum

Everyone knows drums are the heart of all music. If you have an empty coffee can, you have your own drum!

What you'll need

- ☐ coffee can with the plastic lid
- ☐ construction paper
- ☐ crayons, markers or paint
- ☐ tape
- ☐ scissors

1. Cut the construction paper to fit around the coffee can.

2. Decorate your paper.

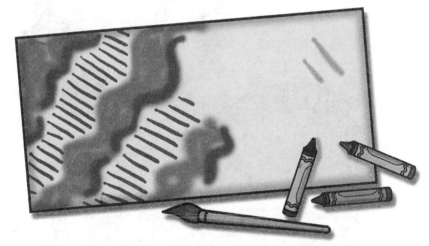

3. Cover the can with the paper and tape it on.

4. Beat rhythms on the lid with your hands.

Suggestion

● Fill a one-pound coffee can with water. Stretch an inner tube over the top tied on tightly with heavy rubber bands. This drum makes a wonderful sound.

Tambourine

Add a little spice to your music! Shake your tambourine for a rattle, and tap the sides for beats.

What you'll need

- [ ] two 9" paper plates
- [ ] crayons, felt-tip pens, watercolors, tempera or acrylic paints
- [ ] jingle bells
- [ ] rice, shelled corn, small pebbles, plastic beads, dried beans or peas
- [ ] yarn, narrow ribbon or pipe cleaners
- [ ] glue
- [ ] paper hole punch

Here's how . . .

1. Color or paint a design on the bottoms of the plates. Let them dry completely.

2. Punch holes about 2 inches apart around the rims. Then, tie a jingle bell at each hole with a length of yarn.

3. Place a handful of rice onto one plate.

4. Glue the paper plates together, rim to rim, with the eating surfaces facing each other.

5. Hold the rims tightly and shake or tap the tambourine.

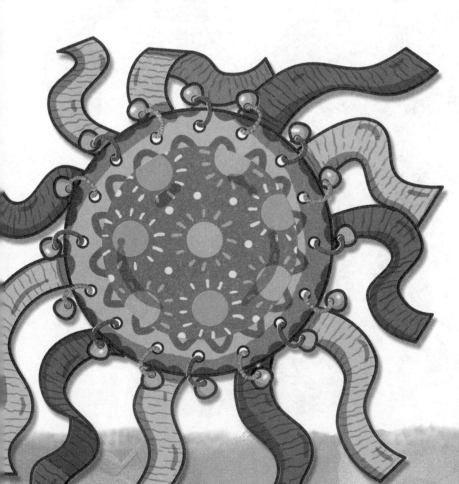

Suggestions

- Use a paper hole punch to make holes, evenly spaced, around the rims. Thread colored pipe cleaners through the holes and twist to secure.

- Cut twelve tissue paper strips (about 1 inch by 9 inches). Glue the ends of the strips between the plates (before step 3) to create streamers.

Shakers

Shakers, or maracas, are popular instruments in many places. Make your own maracas to shake things up!

shake rattle shake

shake rattle shake

Energetic Shaker

Decorate two paper cups. Add dry beans, then tape the two cups together.

Roll Shaker

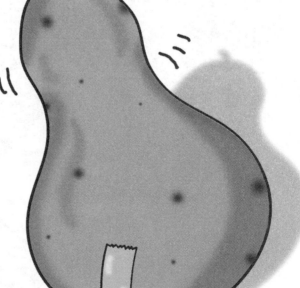

Decorate a cardboard paper towel roll. Fill the roll with beads, rice or dried beans. Seal both ends with cellophane or wax paper, held tight by rubber bands.

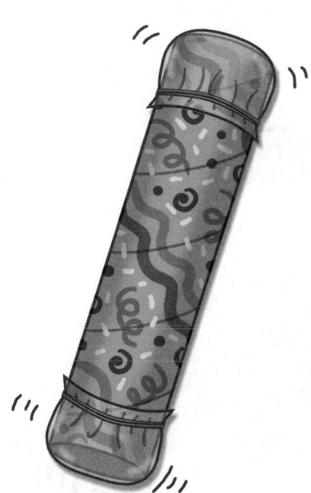

Gourd Maraca

Have an adult cut a small hole in a dried gourd. Put in a little rice, seeds or dry beans. Color a small piece of masking tape, and use it to cover the hole.

Box Guitar

You can make a guitar with things you have around the house! You'll be strumming tunes in no time!

What you'll need

- ☐ a shoebox (no lid needed)
- ☐ rubber bands of varying widths
- ☐ tempera paint
- ☐ paintbrush with stiff bristles
- ☐ paper towel roll
- ☐ glue
- ☐ scissors

1. Paint the paper towel roll and entire shoebox, a few sides at a time, with a dark brown color. Let it dry.

2. Without getting your paintbrush wet, paint over the dark brown with lighter brown paint. This makes it look like wood. Let it dry.

3. Glue the paper towel roll to a short end of the shoebox.

4. Stretch the rubber bands around the open shoebox. Space them out evenly, from the widest to the most narrow band.

5. Experiment by plucking the strings one at a time as well as by strumming the strings all at once.

Musical Glasses

The "glass harmonica" is a real instrument used by some orchestras. See how many tunes you can play!

What you'll need

- ☐ 4–8 identical drinking glasses or glass bottles
- ☐ water

Here's how . . .

1. Fill the glasses with varying amounts of water.

2. Gently rub a clean wet finger around the rim. Each glass makes a different sound.

3. Pour out or add water to some glasses to change their sounds.

4. Make up tunes with your Musical Glasses.

Suggestions

● Another way to play the glasses is to very gently tap the sides of the glasses with a spoon.

● If you use glass bottles, you can make a different sound by blowing across the top of each one. Listen for differences in the sounds made by tapping and those made by blowing.

Rhythm Sticks

Use this simple craft alone or with another instrument you made. See if you can keep the beat to your favorite songs.

What you'll need

☐ 2 dowel rods

Here's how . . .

1. Any local hardware store will have dowel rods in a variety of sizes (widths and lengths). Choose the size you like best. The hardware store may even cut them to the appropriate length (about 1 foot).

2. Beat the sticks together to go along with music.

Suggestions

- Use these with the kid-size drum made on page 72.

- Have an adult saw grooves into one or both of the sticks. Then, you can rub them across each other or beat them together.

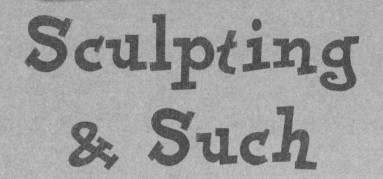

Sculpting & Such

When you create a sculpture, you are making something that is three dimensional. You'll be amazed at the shapes and figures you can create with your hands!

There is no right or wrong way to sculpt. Many artists create figures that look like people or objects they recognize. And many artists create shapes to express how they feel. However you approach it, you should have fun. Remember, you can start over at any time.

You can make your own clay by following the directions in this section. You can make Self-Hardening Clay, Frozen Bread Clay or even Goopy Goo! Clay can be reused for hours and hours of fun. Please note that the recipes are not intended to be edible unless indicated. Also, many recipes call for food coloring, which may stain.

Before you begin, put on some old clothes and cover your work area with wax paper. Then, get ready to make prickly porcupines, beautiful bunnies and perfect pinch pots!

Sand Painting

"Sculpt" with layers of sand! Sand paintings are fun to make and easy to clean up!

What you'll need

- [ ] sand (white sand from garden shops works best)
- [ ] baby food jar or another kind of glass jar with a lid
- [ ] food coloring
- [ ] paper cups
- [ ] spoon

1. Fill paper cups about three-quarters full of sand.

2. Add a few drops of food coloring to each cup and mix well. Prepare at least three different colors of sand.

3. Carefully spoon the sand into the jar, forming one layer of color at a time.

4. When the jar is full, screw on the lid tightly.

Suggestion

● After you fill your jar, take a toothpick and slowly poke into the sand along the sides. This will create wavy lines of different colors without completely mixing them.

Beach Scene

Make a real-looking beach for dolls or action figures. Or use it as a display in your room!

What you'll need

- a shoe box lid
- blue paint
- paintbrush
- sand
- miniature beach items, like twigs, pebbles, shells, grass, paper umbrellas or small toy figures
- spoon
- glue
- fabric scraps (optional)

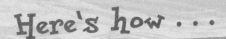

Here's how . . .

1. Paint the inside of the box lid blue.

2. When the paint has dried, add spoonfuls of sand to one-half of the lid to form a "beach."

3. Add twigs, pebbles, shells, grass, small toy figures and other items to make it look like a real beach scene. Use the fabric scraps to make miniature beach towels.

4. Glue everything to keep it in place.

Clotheshanger Clown

You'll have a silly clown "hanging around" when you're done with this project!

What you'll need

- wire clotheshanger
- dessert-sized paper plate or a small construction paper circle
- three 9" x 12" sheets of construction paper
- crayons
- pencil
- glue
- tape
- scissors
- pom-poms, plastic wiggly eyes (optional)

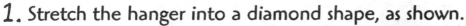

1. Stretch the hanger into a diamond shape, as shown.

2. Color the plate to make a clown face. If desired, add a pom-pom nose and plastic wiggly eyes.

3. Cut out a triangle from construction paper. Make it about 4 inches across and 5 inches tall. If desired, glue a pom-pom to the top point of the hat.

4. Glue the hat to the top of the face. Tape the face onto the hook of the hanger.

5. Fold two sheets of construction paper in half.

6. Trace your hand on one sheet and your foot on the other. You might want to ask someone else to trace for you.

7. Cut through both parts of each folded paper to make two hands and two feet.

8. Tape your cut-out hands and feet in place on the hanger, as shown at left. (Simply turn one cut-out over to get a set of left and right hands and feet.)

9. To hang your clown, attach a few pieces of looped tape in several areas on the back of the paper and stick it to the wall. Or hang it by the hanger hook on a short nail.

Plaster Picture Plaque

Turn one of your favorite pictures into a wall hanging for your room!

What you'll need

- plaster of paris
- color picture cut from a greeting card, calendar or postcard
- clear shellac spray
- one sturdy paper plate (size of plate depends upon size of picture)
- bowl for mixing plaster
- stick for stirring plaster
- sturdy wire (about 1 1/2" long) or large paper clip for the hook
- fine sandpaper
- scissors
- water
- tempera paint (optional)
- an adult

1. Choose a colorful picture from a greeting card, calendar or postcard. Cut or tear the picture to fit the center of the paper plate.

2. Lay the picture facedown in the center of the plate.

3. Pour water into the bowl. The amount of water should be equal to what the plate could hold. If you want colored plaster, add some paint to the water.

4. Add dry plaster of paris slowly into the water until the water no longer absorbs the plaster. Stir the mixture with a stick until the mixture is very thick and smooth like cake batter.

5. Pour the mixture into the plate and over the picture.

6. Before the plaster dries, press in a hook at the top center of the plaque. Most of the hook should be seen above the plaster.

7. When the plaster is completely dry, it will be easy to remove from the paper plate.

8. Sand the rough edges lightly with fine sandpaper.

9. Have an adult help you spray the plaque with a clear shellac to give it a shiny finish. Make sure to do it in an open area.

Leaf Prints

Make natural wall hangings, using leaves, twigs and even sturdy flowers.

What you'll need

- [ ] 2 cups cornstarch
- [ ] 1 1/2 cups flour
- [ ] a leaf
- [ ] wax paper
- [ ] 1 cup warm water
- [ ] spoon
- [ ] rolling pin
- [ ] plastic drinking straw
- [ ] yarn
- [ ] mixing bowl
- [ ] food coloring (optional)

Here's how . . .

1. Mix the cornstarch and flour in a bowl.

2. If desired, add the food coloring to the water.

3. Make a hollow dent in the center, and stir in the warm water a little at a time. Add water until the mixture feels like stiff dough.

4. Mix the dough all together.

5. Knead (press, pull and fold) the mixture on wax paper. Sprinkle it with more flour if the dough is too sticky.

6. Flatten the dough and smooth it out with a rolling pin. Be careful not to roll it out too thin.

7. Place a leaf, veined side down, onto the dough. Press it into the dough with a rolling pin, then remove it carefully.

8. Poke a hole in the top of the dough with a straw.

9. When the print is dry, tie a loop of yarn through the hole to hang it.

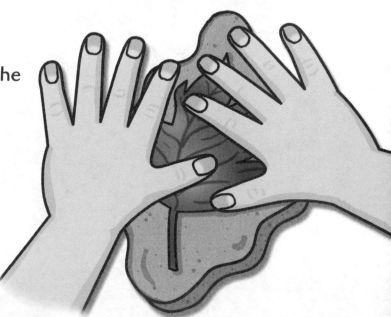

Pinch Pot

If you can pinch, you can make a pinch pot! This project will take several days and by the end, you will have your own piece of pottery!

What you'll need

- [ ] Self-Hardening Clay (see page 99)
- [ ] tempera paint
- [ ] paintbrushes and paint dishes
- [ ] white glue
- [ ] water

Here's how . . .

1. Roll the clay into a ball.

2. Poke your thumb into the center of the ball to make an opening for the pot.

3. Turn the clay in your hand and pinch the opening wider with your thumbs, as shown.

4. Allow the pot to dry for 2 days.

5. When your pot is hardened and completely dry, paint it.

6. When your pot dries again, mix an equal amount of glue and water together.

7. Brush on the mixture to protect the finish of the pot.

Do-It-Yourself Play Clays

Pages 97–101 are recipes for making your own easy-to-use play clay to sculpt as you choose. You might choose to do one instead of another, depending on your own likes and dislikes. Some clays are best for using over and over again. Some clays are better for making projects you want to keep. Two of the clays can even be eaten! Some clays are very firm, while others are very soft. Experiment with all the clays and discover for yourself which is the best one for you! The end of the section gives suggestions for specific things to sculpt with your clay. You can use any clay to make the suggested crafts.

There are certain techniques in working with any clay:

- Rolling the clay is one good way to shape it. You can roll it by moving the clay back and forth on a table or by holding the clay between your hands and rubbing your hands back and forth like when you are trying to get warm.

- You can shape clay with stencils (see page 30). You could press the stencil over flattened clay to imprint the clay. Or squeeze a solid block of clay through a stencil to form a shape.

- Use blocks or other objects to press into flattened clay, much like Object Printing on page 41.

Goopy Goo

Goo is like a liquid clay. It is great to stretch, pull and form your own creations. Be sure to keep it in the bag, and it will stay wet!

Here's how . . .

1. Pour the glue and liquid starch into a plastic bag and seal it.

2. Gently knead (press and squeeze) the bag to mix the ingredients.

3. Add food coloring, if desired, and continue kneading the bag for about 20 minutes. If the mixture still seems thin, add more starch. Add glue if it gets too thick.

4. Store the goo in an airtight plastic bag.

What you'll need

- ❑ 1 cup liquid starch
- ❑ 2 cups white glue
- ❑ resealable plastic bag
- ❑ food coloring (optional)

Play Clay

You can use Play Clay over and over—it will never harden. Make dinosaurs, buildings, people and creatures. Then, squish them together and start over again!

What you'll need

- ☐ 2 cups sifted flour
- ☐ 1 cup salt
- ☐ 6 teaspoons alum*
- ☐ 2 tablespoons salad oil
- ☐ 1 cup water
- ☐ medium-sized mixing bowl and spoon
- ☐ resealable plastic bags or containers
- ☐ food coloring (optional)

  * Alum is found in the baking section of most grocery stores. It acts as a preservative.

Here's how . . .

1. Food coloring may be added to the water before mixing, if color is desired.

2. Mix all materials together in the bowl until they are smooth.

3. The play clay will stay soft for weeks if you keep it in a sealed plastic bag or container.

Suggestion

● See pages 102–104 if you need ideas of what to make with your clay.

Self-Hardening Clay

Create a sculpture you can keep without having to use an oven!

Here's how . . .

1. Mix the salt, flour and alum in a bowl.

2. Add the water gradually to form a ball.

3. Knead (pound, roll and pull) the clay, adding water until it no longer falls apart.

What you'll need

- ☐ 4 cups flour
- ☐ 1 teaspoon alum
- ☐ 1 1/2 cups salt
- ☐ 1 1/2 cups water
- ☐ mixing bowl
- ☐ resealable plastic bag
- ☐ spoon

4. Store in a sealed plastic bag in the refrigerator. Allow the clay to come to room temperature for easy use.

5. Let your finished project dry at room temperature for 2 days. It will become very hard and can be painted.

Suggestion

- See pages 102-104 if you need ideas of what to make with your clay.

Frozen Bread Clay

Mmmm! You can eat this project! Be sure to wash your hands and all working areas before you begin. Hurry! I'm hungry!

What you'll need

- ☐ frozen bread dough, thawed
- ☐ 1 teaspoon cinnamon
- ☐ 1 teaspoon sugar
- ☐ greased cookie sheet
- ☐ oven, preheated to 350°
- ☐ an adult

Here's how . . .

1. Frozen bread dough can be thawed overnight in a refrigerator.

2. Knead (pound, roll and pull) the dough.

3. Shape the dough into letters or other shapes. Make sure each shape is about the same thickness. Otherwise you will burn some parts and undercook others.

4. Sprinkle on them a mixture of the cinnamon and sugar.

5. Place the shaped dough on a greased cookie sheet. Then, have an adult bake it in a 350° oven for 15 to 20 minutes.

6. Let them cool for a few minutes, then eat them.

Peanut Butter Clay

Peanut butter fans will love making, playing with *and* eating this project!

What you'll need

- ☐ 1 cup peanut butter
- ☐ 1 cup nonfat dry milk
- ☐ 1 cup honey
- ☐ mixing bowl and spoon
- ☐ plastic utensils
- ☐ raisins, dry cereal, nuts, chocolate chips (optional)

Here's how . . .

1. Mix the peanut butter, dry milk and honey together in a bowl until it feels like soft dough.

2. Refrigerate your dough for 1 hour.

3. Shape the dough into your own creations.

4. If desired, add raisins, dry cereal, nuts and chocolate chips to make eyes, nose, ears, wings, feet, and so on.

5. Chill them in the refrigerator again, then eat them.

Clay Creations

Now that you have your own clay, there are a million things you can do with it. Here are just a few ideas!

Octopus

Divide your clay in half and make a ball with one half. The other half is for making the eight long legs. You can do this by breaking off pieces and rolling them between your hands or on a flat surface. Set the ball (the body) in the middle of a paper plate and attach each leg by pinching it to the body.

Noodles

Make noodles with clay and a garlic press. Fill the well of the garlic press with clay, then close it to squeeze out strands of clay. Add more clay to lengthen the strands. This technique is also effective for making hair for other clay creatures.

Snowmen

Make three balls of clay in different sizes. Poke a toothpick or a small piece of spaghetti into the largest ball and attach it to the next sized ball. Repeat this step to attach the smallest ball for the head. Use a plastic straw to form eyes and buttons by poking it into the clay. Pieces of uncooked spaghetti or toothpicks can make noses and arms.

Snail

First, roll a long piece of clay. Turn up one end to make the snail's head. Then, roll up the other end to make the snail's shell. Two small pieces of uncooked spaghetti or pipe cleaners can be stuck into the snail's head to make feelers. *(continued on next page)*

Bunny

Roll balls of all sizes to make the bunny's body, tail, cheeks and one tiny ball for the nose. Insert small pieces of spaghetti into the bunny's cheeks for whiskers. Flatten two small pieces of clay to shape the bunny's long ears and pinch them to the head.

Prickly Porcupines

Shape your clay like an egg. Stretch out one end of the "egg" to make the head. Break up uncooked spaghetti and stick them into the porcupine's body. Next, add four pretzel pieces for feet. Add eyes by poking a drinking straw into the clay or pressing beads into the clay.

Robin's Egg Nest

Fill a garlic press with clay and press it closed to make strands. Make a nest with the strands, and make a dent in the middle of it with your thumb. Then, roll two or three little oval shapes for eggs. If you are using Self-Hardening Clay (see page 99), you may want to paint the nests brown or green and the eggs blue when you get to that step.

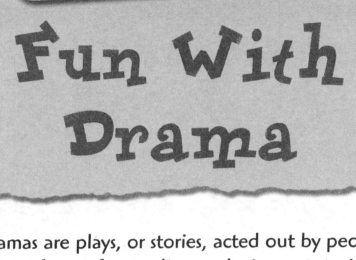

Fun With Drama

Dramas are plays, or stories, acted out by people, usually in front of an audience. Acting out stories can be lots of fun, especially if you use costumes and a little imagination! This section has great ideas for making drama fun and exciting.

Plays often are performed by people in costume, but stories can also be told using puppets. You can make a number of different puppets using the instructions in this section. Some are simple, others are more involved. Decide how you want your character to look and talk and let your imagination go wild! Don't forget to practice "the voice" of the puppet. You can make a puppet sad, silly or serious, just by changing your voice.

Many elements come together when working on a play. The costumes, stage, story and music are just a few. Making, or crafting, each element turns a simple story into art. Plus, you'll be making art twice—once when you make your craft and again when you perform!

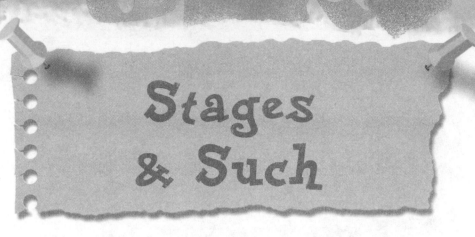

Stages & Such

All the world is a stage, and now you can make your own. Follow these instructions to make a stage for yourself or for a puppet.

Puppet Stage With a Background Set

Place a low table in front of a chalkboard or a large sheet of butcher paper taped to the wall. Draw scenery on the chalkboard behind the table. The table can serve as a stage and the chalkboard as a backdrop for your puppetry. Then, drape a sheet or blanket around the table. Sit beneath the table with your puppets and let the show begin!

A TV Set

To make a TV screen, cut out a rectangular hole in the bottom of a large cardboard box. Draw features such as buttons and decorate the rest of the box. Set the TV on a table that has been draped with a sheet or a blanket. Get behind the box and perform on TV. You can also use the box for puppets.

Dragon Sock Puppet

How do you make a sock talk? Turn it into a puppet! You can make any animal, person or creature imaginable.

What you'll need

- [ ] sock
- [ ] red felt or fabric oval
- [ ] fabric scraps
- [ ] scissors
- [ ] craft glue (try to use glue made especially for fabric)

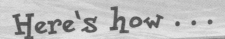

1. Put one hand in the sock to find where the mouth should be. Your thumb should make the bottom jaw of the dragon's mouth.

2. Glue on the red fabric oval where the mouth is formed.

3. Cut out eyes, ears and scales from the fabric scraps, and glue them on the puppet.

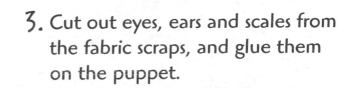

Suggestion

● Have an adult help you sew on the dragon's features so he will last longer. Pin a piece of fabric where you want it, turn the sock inside-out and sew it into place.

King & Queen of Spoons

Plain wooden spoons are a great start to some spectacular puppets! But a cook cannot use these when you are done with them!

What you'll need

- ☐ wooden spoons
- ☐ markers
- ☐ tempera paint
- ☐ paintbrush
- ☐ construction paper or fabric scraps
- ☐ yarn
- ☐ glue

Here's how . . .

1. Paint both spoons with skin color, as shown.

2. When the paint is dry, draw or paint faces on the bowls of the spoons.

3. Glue on yarn hair and construction paper crowns.

4. Wrap construction paper around the handles and glue them on for the puppets' clothes.

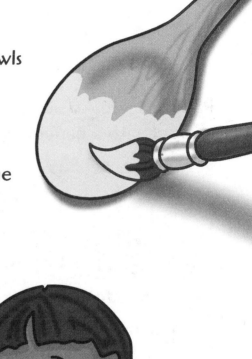

Paper Bag Puppet

Paper bags make puppets that can move on a stick and even talk! Making a puppet with a paper bag is one of the oldest tricks in the book!

What you'll need

- [ ] paper lunch bag
- [ ] newspapers
- [ ] yarn or craft fur
- [ ] dowel rod, wooden spoon or a ruler
- [ ] crayons or markers
- [ ] construction paper
- [ ] glue
- [ ] plastic wiggly eyes (optional)

Here's how . . .

1. Hold the dowel rod in the center of the bag. Fill the bag with crumpled newspaper around the rod, as shown.

2. Tie the bag's opening tightly with yarn. Turn the bag upside down so that the yarn is at the bottom.

3. Using construction paper and crayons, create a face on your puppet.

4. Use yarn to make hair.

Suggestion

● Put your hand inside the bag and make your puppet talk. Decorate it with eyes, hair, a tongue, and so on.

Turkey in the Straw Puppet

Use an ordinary drinking straw to make the turkey come to life. Make several for Thanksgiving decorations!

What you'll need

- brown construction paper
- construction paper scraps
- plastic drinking straw
- feathers
- markers or crayons
- pencil
- stapler
- scissors
- glue
- tape

Here's how . . .

1. Cut the brown construction paper into strips.

2. Make two brown construction paper rings, a large one for the turkey's body and a smaller one for its head. Then, staple them together.

3. Have an adult poke a hole in the bottom of the turkey with a sharp pencil and another hole directly above it where the head and body connect.

4. Stick a straw through both holes.

5. Tape feathers to the back of your turkey.

6. Glue on a construction paper beak and wattle and use markers to draw eyes.

Quick & Easy Puppets

These are some of the fastest puppets you can make!

Greeting Card Puppet

Cut out a person or animal from a greeting card (a used Valentine works well). Glue it onto a plastic drinking straw or a craft stick for an instant puppet.

Cardboard Roll People Puppet

First, draw a face on a cardboard roll. You can add a paper baking cup skirt by cutting out the bottom of a cup, then gluing it to the roll. Glue on yarn or cotton balls for hair and baking cups or paper scraps for hats and other simple features.

Envelope Shark Puppet

Seal a business size (long) envelope. Cut a triangle from one of the short edges to make a mouth. Tape the triangle to the top to be the fin. Trim off the edge of the envelope opposite the mouth, making an opening for your hand. Decorate your shark with eyes, stripes and of course, sharp teeth.

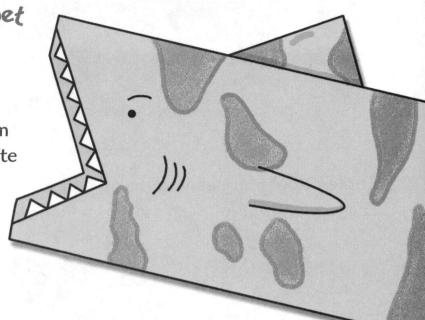

Paper Plate Puppet

Glue or draw a face onto a paper plate. You may want to use yarn hair, button eyes, ribbon eyebrows, and so on. When all is dry, tape a wooden paint stirring stick to the back of the plate.

Craft Stick Puppets

These puppets are easy to make, easy to store and easy to use. Make an army, a zoo, a classroom or even your own family! The sky's the limit!

What you'll need

- ☐ small cardboard roll
- ☐ white paper
- ☐ scissors
- ☐ craft stick
- ☐ crayons or markers
- ☐ tape
- ☐ pom-poms, rickrack, construction paper scraps or other decorative items (optional)
- ☐ glue (optional)

Here's how . . .

1. Cover the cardboard roll with white paper, and tape it on.

2. Add features with crayons and/or other decorative items.

3. Tape a craft stick securely inside the bottom of the roll for the handle. It works best if you tape it in two places.

Suggestions

● Use a wooden paint stirring stick to make larger puppets.

● Draw your own character onto the craft stick.

● Try making an astronaut's space suit with aluminum foil.

Felt Hand Puppet

Learn to sew, and make a puppet at the same time! These puppets are soft and easy to move on your hand.

What you'll need

- ☐ 2 felt pieces, about 5" x 7"
- ☐ felt scraps of another color
- ☐ yarn
- ☐ white paper
- ☐ thread
- ☐ needle
- ☐ pins
- ☐ pencil
- ☐ chalk or pencil for fabric
- ☐ glue
- ☐ scissors

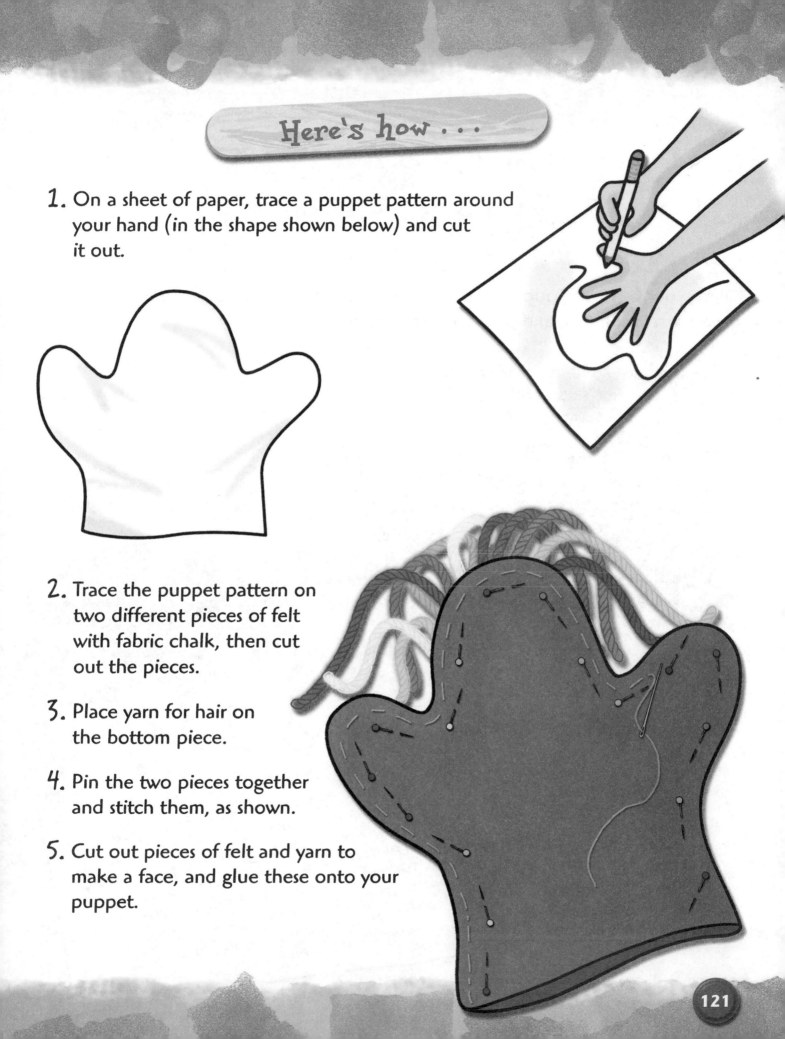

1. On a sheet of paper, trace a puppet pattern around your hand (in the shape shown below) and cut it out.

2. Trace the puppet pattern on two different pieces of felt with fabric chalk, then cut out the pieces.

3. Place yarn for hair on the bottom piece.

4. Pin the two pieces together and stitch them, as shown.

5. Cut out pieces of felt and yarn to make a face, and glue these onto your puppet.

Paper Plate Hand Puppet

With your help, this puppet seems like it's really talking! Add buttons, beads, even macaroni, to make your puppet extra special.

What you'll need

- ☐ two 9" paper plates
- ☐ watercolors, tempera or acrylic paints, or felt-tip pens
- ☐ paintbrush
- ☐ white glue
- ☐ scissors

Suggested trims:
buttons, beads, sections of egg cartons, bottle caps, foam balls, plastic wiggly eyes, paper nut cups, cardboard roll, cork, pieces of sponge, thread spool, paper cup, plastic cup, pom-poms, beans, "popcorn" packing foam, macaroni, yarn, curled gift ribbon, fur, raffia, cotton, fiberfill, construction paper or crepe paper strips, pipe cleaners, broom straws, drinking straws, fabric trims, sequins, foil, paper doilies, veiling, feathers, old costume jewelry

Here's how . . .

1. Fold a 9-inch paper plate in half to form a large mouth.

2. Cut the other paper plate in half.

3. Glue the rim of the halved plate to the rim of the folded plate, leaving the cut edge of the plate unglued and forming a place for your hand, as shown. Note: Do not try to stick your hand in until the glue is completely dry.

4. Use your imagination as you glue some of the suggested trims to the paper plates to make the face. Be careful not to add yarn, feathers or other such items that may accidentally get paint on them. These can be glued in place after the paint is dry.

5. Paint your puppet, then let it dry.

6. Add the trims that do not need painting.

7. Cut a 1 inch by 3 inch strip from the paper plate scrap and glue it to the folded plate, as shown. This will give you a thumb hold, so that you will be better able to open and close the mouth of the puppet.

Box Prop

Perform a play that is out of this world with your own rocket! Or just pretend you're defending a royal castle or floating down a moat.

What you'll need

- ☐ large appliance box and/or moving boxes
- ☐ pencil
- ☐ masking or duct tape
- ☐ utility knife
- ☐ glue
- ☐ scissors
- ☐ paint, markers, construction paper, wrapping paper, fabric, foil, clear plastic (optional)
- ☐ an adult

1. Plan a type of transportation or building to make. Place the boxes where you want them.

2. Draw windows and doors where you want them.

3. Have an adult cut out your windows and doors as well as the walls between the boxes to connect them. Make sure any flaps are tucked in tightly. Or have the adult cut the flaps off the boxes.

4. Tape the boxes to keep them together.

5. Decorate your creation.

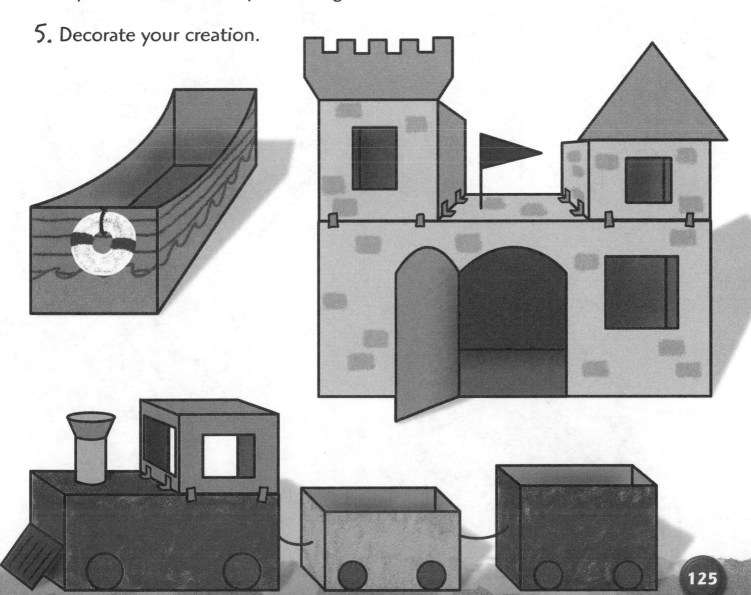

Costumes

When you wear a costume, you can be anything you want—a dinosaur, a princess or even a monster!

What you'll need

- ☐ grocery bag or pillowcase
- ☐ glue or a needle and thread
- ☐ crayons, paint or fabric
- ☐ scissors
- ☐ an adult

Here's how...

1. Cut an opening for your head at the closed end of the bag, as shown.

2. Cut out arm openings on the sides.

3. Decorate your costume. Use crayons, paint or fabric to add details.

Costume Masks

Masks aren't just for Halloween! They can be used all year for parties, parades, plays and for "dress-up"—you can become any character you want to be.

What you'll need

- two 9" paper plates
- crayons, felt-tip pens, watercolors, tempera or acrylic paints
- construction paper in different colors
- nylon stocking (a 1" x 9" strip for securing the mask to your head)
- white glue
- scissors
- pencil
- stapler
- craft knife
- an adult

Suggested materials:

paint, yarn, craft fur, rags, raffia, unraveled rope, cotton, string, curled construction paper, steel wool, fiberfill, curled gift-wrap ribbon, paint, pipe cleaners (for antennae, insert them into foam balls), broom straws, paper strips, drinking straws, yarn or string stiffened with glue, feathers, old costume jewelry, paper or plastic flowers, craft knife (for the adult to use)

Here's how . . .

1. Press one paper plate inside out and hold it against your face. With a crayon, gently mark the areas for your eyes and nose.

2. Have an adult use a craft knife to cut out circles for your eyes and a triangle for your nose. Note: Be sure the openings for the eyes are large enough for full vision.

3. Use the triangular cutout piece as a pattern for the nose. Trace three triangles side by side on the other paper plate. Add 1/4-inch tabs, as shown.

4. Cut out the base of the nose. Fold down the two center lines and fold the tabs out, as shown.

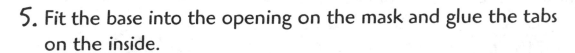

5. Fit the base into the opening on the mask and glue the tabs on the inside.

6. Color or paint the mask. Paint will help the ragged edges on the eye holes look better. Let it dry. *(continued on next page)*

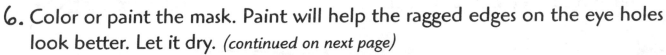

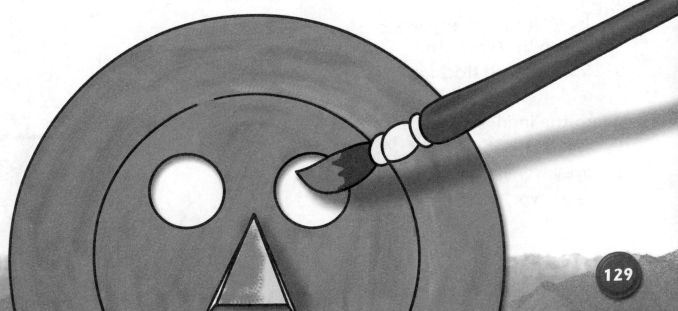

7. From construction paper, cut out a nose shape for the character you want to make and glue it to the base. Look to the right to get some ideas for nose shapes.

8. Cut ears from construction paper and glue them in place. One basic shape can make several kinds of ears. By changing the location of the ears, a face can become a dog, bear, rabbit, cat or person, as shown.

9. Paint or glue on a mouth cut from construction paper. For eyelashes, fringe a strip of construction paper and curl the lashes over a pencil. Glue only one end so they will stand out.

10. To wear your mask, cut a 1 inch by 9 inch strip from a nylon stocking and staple the ends to the inside of your mask at eye level, as shown.

Homemade Toys

Toys have been around for as long as there have been children. Homemade toys combine the enjoyment of games and toys with the satisfaction of making something creative, colorful and fun!

Many of the toys are activities that can be used by one person, such as the Ball and Cup Game and the Creepy Crawler. Other projects are playthings you can use with toys you already have, such as the Clothespin Critters and the Box Castle.

When you have completed making one of the Homemade Toys, you will not only have a new toy or plaything but you'll have something you can display or give as a gift!

Ball & Cup Game

Play this game alone or with another player. Each player gets ten tries. The one who catches the ball the most times, wins!

What you'll need

- 3 oz. paper cup
- yarn
- 12" square of aluminum foil
- 1" × 2" strip of construction paper
- masking tape
- drawing compass or straightened paper clip
- scissors
- ruler

1. Using a compass point, puncture a hole in the bottom of the cup.

2. Cut off about 14 inches of yarn to start and tie a knot at one end. The longer your yarn, the more difficult it will be to catch the ball.

3. Tie a knot at one end of the yarn. Thread the yarn from the inside of the cup so the knot is in the cup.

4. Tape the knot in place for added strength.

5. Fold the strip of construction paper in half lengthwise and twist it at the center.

6. Tie the yarn to the center twist. This will become the center of the ball.

7. Firmly squeeze and shape the strip into a ball.

8. Place the ball into the center of the piece of aluminum foil.

9. Gather the foil around the ball, squeezing and shaping the foil to make a ball shape. Be careful to keep the yarn out of the foil.

10. Hold the cup while swinging the ball. Try to catch the ball in the cup.

Teddy's Train

Choo-choo! Coming through! Make an old-fashioned mini-train for your stuffed animals.

What you'll need

- [ ] rectangular facial tissue boxes
- [ ] yarn
- [ ] paper hole punch
- [ ] colored paper, paint, crayons or markers
- [ ] scissors
- [ ] ruler

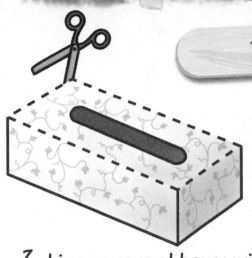

Here's how . . .

1. Cut off the tops of the tissue boxes (or have an adult do it for you).

2. Decorate each box with colored paper, paint, markers, etc.

3. Line up several boxes with the short sides facing each other.

4. Punch two holes at both ends of every box (except the one at the back end. This box needs two holes punched at one end only). The holes should be about 3 inches apart.

5. Thread 8-inch pieces of yarn through the holes to attach the boxes. Tie a knot in each end once the yarn is through each hole.

6. To make a handle to pull the train, thread a 5-foot piece of yarn through both holes in the first box and knot both ends.

7. Put dolls and stuffed animals into the boxes as passengers. Then, pull the train around the room.

Suggestion

● Add paper baking cups for wheels and other cardboard rolls or boxes to make it look more like a train.

Bubbles

You can have your own endless supply of bubbles—and just think, you can make them anytime you want!

What you'll need

- ☐ 1/2 cup glycerine (may be bought at a pharmacy)
- ☐ 1/2 cup water
- ☐ 1 tablespoon liquid dishwashing detergent
- ☐ glass jar with a lid
- ☐ bubble pipe, bubble wand, plastic drinking straws, twist ties, slotted spoons or clotheshangers
- ☐ baking pan (optional)

Here's how . . .

1. Mix all the ingredients in a jar.

2. Make bubble wands out of twist ties, slotted spoons, clotheshangers or straws.

3. Pour some of the bubble mix into a baking pan if you are making larger bubbles.

4. You can reuse the bubbles as long as you keep the jar tightly closed when you are done playing.

Me Doll

Now, you'll always have a friend around for company—yourself! Make a whole set showing your many different sides!

What you'll need

- ☐ poster board or stiff construction paper
- ☐ pencil
- ☐ crayons, markers or paint
- ☐ 13 paper fasteners (brads)
- ☐ scissors
- ☐ yarn, fabric scraps, other small decorative materials (optional)

Here's how . . .

1. Draw an oval the size of an egg on the poster board and cut it out. This is the head.

2. Draw and cut out another oval, this one being the size of a small envelope (with its corners rounded off). This is the body.

3. Draw and cut out 8 more long ovals about 4 inches long. These are parts of arms and legs.

4. Draw and cut out 2 hand shapes and 2 foot shapes, each about 1 inch long.

5. Color, draw or paint your own face, clothes you might wear and other details where they belong.

body (1)

head (1)

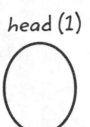

arms and legs (8)

hands (2)   feet (2)

6. Attach the parts with paper fasteners to make a body that moves, as shown.

7. If desired, add yarn for hair, fabric for clothing or more materials for other details.

Suggestions

- Use a school picture to glue onto the head to show your own face.

- Glue a paint stirrer or dowel rods to the back of your Me Doll to make a puppet that moves.

Clothespin Critters

You can make pictures of your favorite animals stand up on their own! Let your imagination—and these animals—run wild in your own zoo, rainforest or circus!

What you'll need

- ☐ clip-on clothespins
- ☐ coloring books or magazines
- ☐ construction paper or poster board
- ☐ crayons
- ☐ feathers, yarn, pom-poms or stickers
- ☐ scissors
- ☐ glue

Here's how . . .

1. Cut out animal pictures from a coloring book, trimming off the legs. Color the animals.

2. Glue the pictures onto the construction paper and trim the edges.

3. Decorate the pictures by gluing on feathers, yarn (for manes) and pom-poms (for tails), or by using round stickers (for spots).

4. Attach the clothespins to make your animals stand.

Suggestion

● Make backdrops or shadowboxes for your clothespin critters using construction paper or shoeboxes. Decorate with crayons, markers or paint to create the climate where your critters are found.

Box Castle

Make a decorated castle for your action figures, using boxes from your kitchen!

What you'll need

- ☐ empty boxes from cereal, oatmeal, salt and other products
- ☐ cardboard paper towel rolls
- ☐ construction paper
- ☐ paper baking cups
- ☐ glue
- ☐ tape
- ☐ scissors

1. Tape the paper onto the rolls and boxes.

2. Group them into a castle shape.

3. Cut out construction paper for doors and windows and glue them on.

4. Glue paper baking cups to the tops of the roll towers and along the top of the castle.

Suggestions

● Cut a section out of the castle wall to make a door that swings out.

● Paint the paper to look like a castle wall.

● Make flags out of construction paper and toothpicks. Attach the flags to the tops of the castle towers.

● Have an adult use hot glue to make your castle more durable.

Floating Boat

With a little help from an adult, you can make this boat that really floats! It's perfect for the bathtub, or maybe even a pond.

What you'll need

- ☐ 2-liter plastic soda bottle
- ☐ craft stick
- ☐ construction paper
- ☐ play clay or modeling clay
- ☐ stickers
- ☐ glue
- ☐ scissors
- ☐ an adult

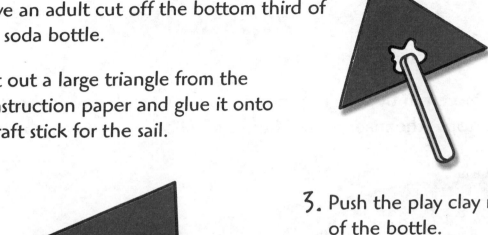

1. Have an adult cut off the bottom third of the soda bottle.

2. Cut out a large triangle from the construction paper and glue it onto a craft stick for the sail.

3. Push the play clay into the center of the bottle.

4. Stick the sail into the play clay.

5. Decorate the outside of your boat with colorful stickers.

6. Float your boat in the bathtub.

Suggestion

● Your action figures should fit perfectly in the boat.

Travel Tic-Tac-Toe

Make a long trip more fun by bringing your own game. Don't worry about sharp curves and quick stops—the magnets will hold the pieces on the gameboard!

What you'll need

- ☐ magnetic sheet
- ☐ 4 craft sticks
- ☐ 5 buttons, bottle caps or other small, round objects
- ☐ cardboard or poster board
- ☐ tissue paper
- ☐ resealable plastic bag
- ☐ scissors
- ☐ glue
- ☐ ruler
- ☐ an adult

1. Cut both the magnetic sheet and cardboard into a square with 4 1/2 inch sides. Peel off the white paper and stick the magnetic sheet to the cardboard.

2. Decorate the side of the cardboard that shows. This is the bottom of your gameboard.

3. Glue the craft sticks to make the Tic-Tac-Toe gameboard on the magnetic square.

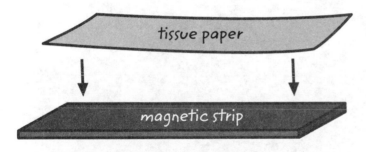

tissue paper

magnetic strip

4. To make the X's, have an adult help you cut a magnetic strip about 1 inch long and 5 inches wide. Take the paper off and fit the tissue paper, trimmed to the same size, to the sticky side. Then, cut the magnet into 1/4- to 1/2-inch wide strips, as shown. Glue the magnet strips together to make 5 X's.

5. To make the O's, have an adult help you cut 5 magnet pieces (any shape) smaller than the buttons. Glue the paper side to the buttons.

6. Keep the X's, O's and gameboard in a resealable plastic bag.

Creepy Crawler

This funny furry creature really rolls! Have an adult help you with the wire cutters so you can have a Creepy Crawler of your own!

What you'll need

- [ ] 1 paper or foam soup bowl
- [ ] craft fur or a thin rug remnant
- [ ] wire clotheshanger
- [ ] 2 thread spools
- [ ] 6 pipe cleaners
- [ ] white glue or tape
- [ ] paper hole punch
- [ ] wire cutters
- [ ] scissors
- [ ] ruler
- [ ] felt or paper for eyes or plastic wiggly eyes (optional)
- [ ] an adult

1. Cut the rim off the bowl, as shown, to make the body.

2. Have an adult help you use the wire cutters to cut a 7-inch piece of wire from the clotheshanger.

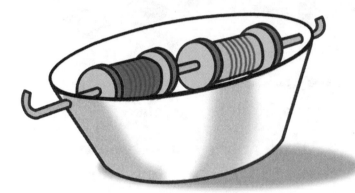

3. Punch a hole on each side of the bowl about 1/2 inch from the top.

4. Insert one end of the wire into one of the holes in the bowl, thread on two spools for wheels and push the wire out the hole on the opposite side.

5. Bend the ends of the wire upward to hold it in place, as shown.

6. For legs, punch three small holes on each side of the bowl and stick a pipe cleaner through each hole, as shown.

7. Tape or glue the legs in place inside the bowl.

8. Shape each pipe cleaner to form a leg, including the knee and foot.

(continued on next page)

9. Turn the bowl upside down and glue a circle of craft fur over the bowl.

10. Glue on the eyes.

11. Roll your Creepy Crawler down a slope (like an empty driveway) or give him a little push to start him rolling.

Suggestions

● Have an adult use hot glue to make it more durable.

● Attach a long string or piece of yarn to the wire. Now, you can pull your Creepy Crawler behind you!

Mixed Materials

The crafts in this section use many kinds of materials. When you mix different media, or materials, you can get some really neat results! Combining the leaves and twigs you find outside with paint, or something from the kitchen, can produce unusual projects that will grab everyone's attention!

Most of the materials for these projects can be found around your house. And some of the materials can be found outside, in nature. Searching for nature materials can be half the fun! You never know what you'll discover as you look for materials to make your Leaf Rubbing, Rock Paperweight or Gumdrop Tree. Have fun!

Rainbow Yarn Picture

Give someone a rainbow on a rainy day! This rainbow makes a perfect wall hanging or a great greeting card!

What you'll need

- [ ] yarn in all the colors of the rainbow (red, orange, yellow, green, blue and purple)
- [ ] white glue
- [ ] light blue construction paper
- [ ] cotton balls
- [ ] scissors
- [ ] liquid starch (optional)

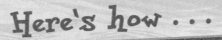

1. Cut equal lengths of each color of yarn.

2. Dip a piece of yarn in the starch (use glue if you do not have starch). Wipe off the extra liquid, as shown. Do the same for each color.

3. Place the yarn on light blue paper to form a rainbow.

4. When all the yarn is in place, glue on the cotton to form a cloud.

Suggestion

- If your rainbow is a full arch, the pieces of yarn will have to be different lengths. The top color will be much longer than the bottom color. Lay out the rainbow before cutting and gluing the yarn.

153

Rock Paperweight

Do you collect rocks on the beach or in the woods? Make them useful and turn them into natural paperweights!

What you'll need

- [ ] rock
- [ ] paints
- [ ] paintbrushes
- [ ] paint dishes
- [ ] water
- [ ] soap
- [ ] shellac or watered-down white glue

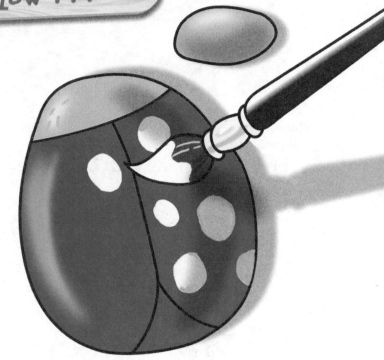

Here's how . . .

1. Scrub the rock clean with soap and water. Let it dry.

2. Paint a picture on it. If you do not want the colors to run into each other, let the paint dry in between coats.

3. Shellac your rock when the paint dries.

Suggestion

● Painting a face or a body on your rock could make it a new "pet."

Lacing Cards

Everyone loves working with Lacing Cards! Make these yourself or have an adult make them for *you* to use.

What you'll need

- ☐ squares of poster board
- ☐ drawing compass
- ☐ yarn
- ☐ masking tape
- ☐ pencil
- ☐ an adult

Here's how . . .

1. Draw a simple design on the poster board square.

2. Have an adult punch holes along the outline of the design, using the drawing compass.

3. Wrap 1–2 inches of masking tape around the yarn to form a needle. Tie a knot in the other end.

4. Lace the yarn through the holes to make your picture.

5. You can go back around the card to make a solid line, or just stop after one time around for the dotted line.

Teddy Bear

You can make Goldilocks's very own Three Bears, just using paper bags!

What you'll need

- ☐ brown paper grocery bag
- ☐ newspaper, tissue paper or scrap paper
- ☐ crayons
- ☐ stapler
- ☐ scissors

1. Draw a bear shape on a bag and cut it out.

2. Trace the bear shape on the other side of the bag, and cut it out, as shown.

3. Color a face onto one bear shape. Draw a tail on the other shape.

4. Staple the bears together along the edges, leaving the tops of the heads open. Make sure any writing on the bag is to the inside where it won't be seen.

5. Stuff the bear with newspaper or tissue paper.

6. Staple the top of the head shut.

Suggestion

● Make a zoo with other "stuffed" animals.

Leaf Rubbing

If you're into collecting leaves, this project is for you! If you make this in the fall, be sure to use fresh, not dry, leaves!

What you'll need

- ☐ fresh leaves
- ☐ tissue paper
- ☐ construction paper in light colors
- ☐ crayons
- ☐ liquid starch, watered-down white glue or polymer gel
- ☐ paintbrush
- ☐ newspaper
- ☐ scissors

Here's how . . .

1. Cut the tissue paper and construction paper into 5-inch squares.

2. Cover your work space with newspaper.

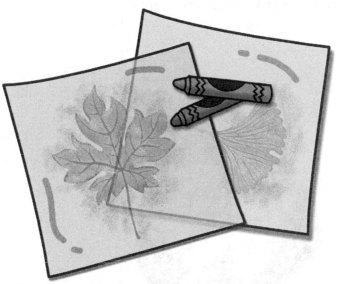

3. Place a leaf on your work space with the vein side up.

4. Put a square of tissue paper over the leaf and rub gently with the side of a crayon until a leaf vein pattern appears.

5. Cut out the shape of the leaf.

6. Take a construction paper square and brush it with liquid starch.

7. Place the tissue paper with the leaf print on top of the construction paper and brush the paper again with the starch. Then, let your rubbing dry.

8. Do the same to each of your collected leaves.

Suggestion

- Cut out the leaf shapes and make a separate collage with them.

Sand Garden

Make your own Sand Garden! Decorate it with unusual stones, or press objects into the sand for a creative effect.

What you'll need

- ☐ sand
- ☐ large baking pan
- ☐ heavy cardboard
- ☐ water
- ☐ scissors

Here's how . . .

1. Fill the pan almost to the top with sand.

2. Add enough water to dampen the sand.

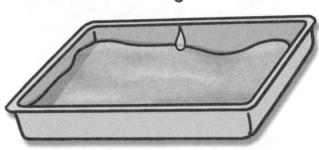

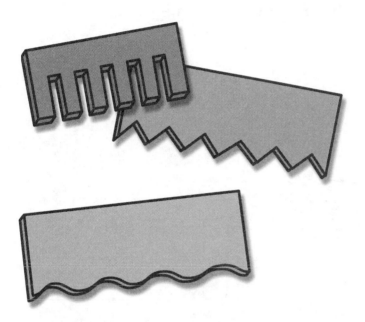

3. Cut out rectangular pieces of cardboard.

4. Cut an interesting edge on one side of each rectangle. Vary the edges by using straight, curved or zigzagged cuts.

5. Move the cardboard "comb" across the sand to make patterns.

Suggestion

● Draw lines and circles in the sand using twigs, plastic spoons or craft sticks. Also use plastic containers, cookie cutters or other objects to press into the sand.

Tulip Pot

Now, you can watch your own spring tulip "grow" any time of year!

What you'll need

- [ ] foam cup
- [ ] tongue depressor or craft stick
- [ ] construction paper
- [ ] glue
- [ ] scissors
- [ ] pencil

1. Draw the outline of a tulip on the paper. Make sure it is smaller than the cup. Cut it out.

2. Glue the tulip on the top of a tongue depressor, as shown.

3. Cut a slit in the bottom of the foam cup. The slit should be large enough for the tongue depressor.

4. Hold the cup. Pull the tongue depressor through the cup far enough so you cannot see the flower in the pot.

5. Make your flower grow by slowly pushing the tongue depressor up.

Suggestion

● Make other flower pots using different flowers.

Nature Pictures

Make a memory of your nature walk or adventure, frame and hang it on the wall!

What you'll need

- [ ] variety of seeds, dried weeds, leaves, twigs, pebbles, acorns, buds, nuts, etc.
- [ ] chipboard or plywood
- [ ] varnish or shellac
- [ ] glue
- [ ] hammer
- [ ] thumbtack or nail
- [ ] hook for hanging
- [ ] old paintbrush
- [ ] an adult

Here's how . . .

1. Have an adult help you hammer the hook into the back of the chipboard, as shown.

2. Arrange and glue all the natural supplies to the front of the chipboard.

3. Glue sticks around the edges to make a frame.

4. Coat the front with a clear varnish.

Foil Design

Make your own creativity "shine" with this one-of-a-kind project!

What you'll need

- [ ] aluminum foil
- [ ] cardboard
- [ ] permanent felt-tipped markers (water-based markers will not work)
- [ ] yarn
- [ ] glue
- [ ] tape
- [ ] scissors
- [ ] ruler

1. Cut the cardboard into a 10-inch square.

2. Cover the entire square with aluminum foil. Fold the extra foil around the edges and tape it down on the back.

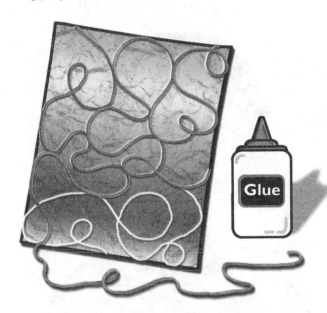

3. Use glue to draw a design on the square.

4. Lay yarn on top of the glue design.

5. Use the markers to color each section of your design a different color.

Suggestions

● For a different look, glue the yarn down *before* putting the foil on the cardboard.

● Use colored glue.

Flower Vase

Use this vase for dried or paper flowers. Decorate it with brightly colored paper to make it look just like stained glass!

What you'll need

- ☐ round cardboard box (such as oatmeal or bread crumb boxes)
- ☐ colored paper, wallpaper or wrapping paper
- ☐ old paintbrush
- ☐ glue
- ☐ scissors

Here's how . . .

1. Cut or tear the paper into small pieces about the same shape.

2. Decorate the box by gluing pieces of the colored paper over the entire box.

3. Brush glue over the whole vase to smooth it out.

Suggestions

- Use the flowers from the Spring Flowers project on page 16.

- Use masking tape to cover the box, then rub it all with shoe polish to give it the look of leather.

Elephant

The circus is coming! That's what people will think when you make this roly-poly elephant.

What you'll need

- [ ] round cardboard oatmeal box and its lid
- [ ] construction paper
- [ ] 4 cardboard toilet paper rolls
- [ ] crayons or markers
- [ ] paint
- [ ] yarn
- [ ] tape
- [ ] glue
- [ ] scissors
- [ ] paintbrush

1. Use the box with the lid on for the body of the elephant.

2. Cut out the trunk and ears from construction paper. Tape them to the body.

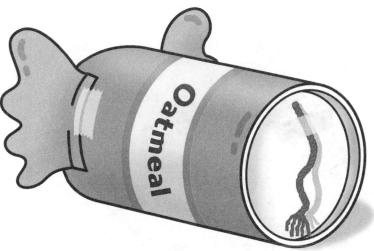

3. Tape a piece of yarn to the top of the box for a tail, as shown.

4. Cut the toilet paper rolls to fit to the body and to keep your elephant standing level, as shown. Glue them on for legs. You may need to hold them in place until they dry.

5. Paint your elephant gray and add eyes and other features.

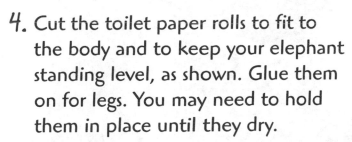

Gumdrop Tree

You won't find this tree growing in the forest! It makes a great table display, and you'll get to eat the leftover gumdrops!

What you'll need

- [ ] gumdrops
- [ ] small branch of a tree or bush
- [ ] clay or sand
- [ ] drinking cup
- [ ] paint
- [ ] paintbrush

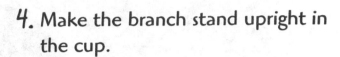

Here's how . . .

1. Fill the cup with clay.

2. Strip the leaves off the branch.

3. Paint a design on the cup.

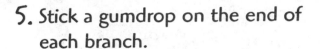

4. Make the branch stand upright in the cup.

5. Stick a gumdrop on the end of each branch.

GUMDROPS

Bug Out

Is it a prehistoric insect? A rare and deadly bug? Or just something silly from your imagination? You decide.

What you'll need

- ☐ crayons
- ☐ various natural objects—such as leaves, twigs, small pine cones or tree bark
- ☐ construction paper
- ☐ glue

Here's how . . .

1. Sort through your collection of natural objects. Arrange them in different ways to make different kinds of bugs.

2. Draw the background on construction paper. Include details to show where the insect lives and what it eats. Ideas may be scientifically correct or artistically inventive.

3. Glue the insect to the background paper.

Suggestion

- Arrange and glue the leftover natural objects to the background.

Dry Food Collage

This picture features textures. Use rough, smooth, large, small, curved and straight dry food pieces.

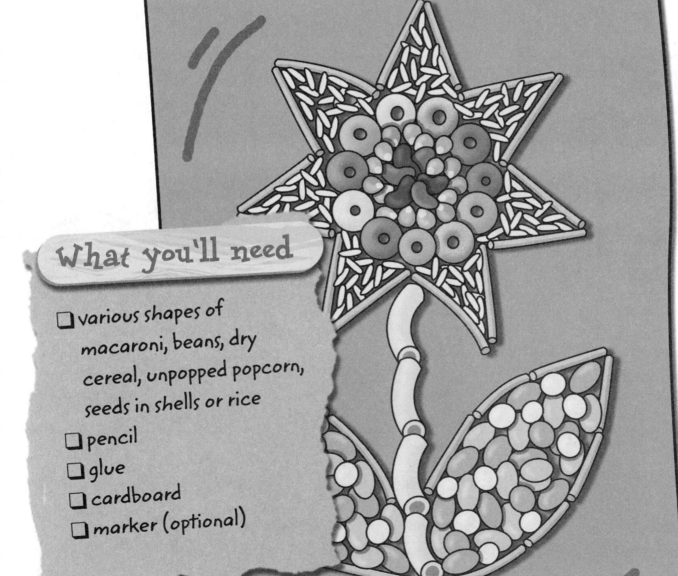

What you'll need

- ☐ various shapes of macaroni, beans, dry cereal, unpopped popcorn, seeds in shells or rice
- ☐ pencil
- ☐ glue
- ☐ cardboard
- ☐ marker (optional)

1. Lightly draw a design or picture on the cardboard.

2. Dab small glue dots on the design. Do not dab more than six to eight dots at a time or the glue will dry.

3. Place the macaroni on top of the glue dots to outline your design. Trace your design using the marker, if desired.

4. Put glue inside the design.

5. Fill in the design with other dry food items to create texture.

Homemade Scrapbook

Create your own scrapbook of memories! Put photos, ticket stubs, cards and more in this attractive book designed by you.

What you'll need

- [ ] blank scrapbook, photo album or journal
- [ ] solid, light-colored fabric
- [ ] fabric paints, fabric markers or permanent markers
- [ ] acid-free paper or construction paper
- [ ] glue
- [ ] scissors
- [ ] ruler (optional)
- [ ] decorative objects, such as buttons, rickrack, ribbon, sequins, plastic gems, glitter, etc.

Here's how . . .

1. Measure out the fabric to fit the size of your book. Cut it out 2–3 inches bigger all around, as shown.

2. Cover the front of your book with glue. Letting the extra fabric hang off the edges, place the fabric on the front. Smooth the fabric over the cover to get rid of any air pockets.

3. Cover the spine (the narrow mid-section) and the back with glue. Smooth the fabric over the spine, then cut off only the extra fabric from the spine. Close the book.

4. Smooth the fabric over the back of the book. Let the glue dry.

glue paper here

5. Cover the inside parts of the extra fabric with dabs of glue. Fold the extra fabric into the inside of the cover as you would fold wrapping paper. Make it as flat as possible.

6. Cut 2 sheets of paper just a little smaller than the front. Cover one side of each sheet with glue. Glue 1 sheet over the inside front cover and 1 over the inside back cover. This hides the extra fabric.

7. Decorate the cover with decorative objects. Outline your design and write your name with fabric paints.

Sun, Moon & Stars Mobile

Make this mobile, and watch the sky twirl above your head!

What you'll need

- [ ] construction paper or heavier paper in sun, moon and stars colors
- [ ] yarn
- [ ] wire clotheshanger
- [ ] cardboard paper towel roll
- [ ] crayons or markers
- [ ] white glue
- [ ] gold glitter
- [ ] silver glitter
- [ ] paper hole punch
- [ ] scissors
- [ ] paints and paintbrush (optional)

Here's how . . .

1. Cut the paper into two each of sun, moon and star shapes.

2. Cover one side of each shape with a thin coat of glue.

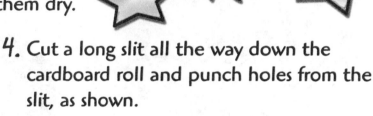

3. Sprinkle gold glitter onto the suns, silver on the stars and moons. Let them dry.

4. Cut a long slit all the way down the cardboard roll and punch holes from the slit, as shown.

5. If desired, paint the roll.

6. Cut 3 pieces of yarn.

7. Knot each piece of yarn several times until the knot is bigger than the hole. Pull each piece of yarn through a hole in the roll (with the knot keeping the yarn in place).

8. Slide the roll onto the clotheshanger and twist it so the holes are at the bottom.

9. Sandwich each yarn end between the tops of the two shapes which are back to back.

10. Glue the shapes together so the yarn cannot be pulled out.

11. Hang your mobile in a breezy place.

Aquarium

There is something "fishy" about this project—your friends will think it's a real aquarium!

What you'll need

- [ ] 9" x 12" white drawing paper
- [ ] 10" x 12" piece of cellophane or plastic wrap
- [ ] 1/2" x 12" strip of black construction paper
- [ ] two 1/2" x 10" strips of black construction paper
- [ ] blue tempera paint
- [ ] construction paper
- [ ] water
- [ ] crayons
- [ ] paintbrush
- [ ] double-sided tape
- [ ] glue
- [ ] scissors

1. Color a scene on the drawing paper with fish and plants that might be in an aquarium. Press hard.

2. Mix water into the blue paint and brush it over your entire picture.

3. When your paint dries, place two 1/2-inch pieces of double-sided tape at the corners and in the center of the bottom edge of the background paper, as shown.

4. Place cellophane over the background paper and press it into place. The cellophane will extend above the top edge of the background paper, giving the illusion of a glass tank.

5. Again, tape over the same areas as in step 3.

6. Glue the black strips over the tape to complete the illusion of an aquarium.

Paper Plate Parade

You won't believe how many animals you can make using simple paper plates! Use these examples or use your own ideas.

What you'll need

- [ ] paper plates in different sizes and colors
- [ ] crayons, felt-tip pens, watercolors, tempera or acrylic paints
- [ ] self-adhesive picture mounts or yarn for hanging
- [ ] pencil
- [ ] ruler
- [ ] scissors
- [ ] white glue
- [ ] pipe cleaners, drinking straws or yarn (optional)
- [ ] plastic wiggly eyes, craft feathers, muffin cups (optional)

Butterfly

Glue two large plates and two small plates overlapping each other. Add a pipe cleaner for the body and antennae. Then, decorate it with paint and glitter or salt (see page 237).

Owl

Use one paper plate with rippled, not smooth, edges. Cut out and glue together, as shown. Color or add a face and craft feathers, if desired.

Fish

Use one large plate and two smaller plates. Cut a sliver of a moon from both the large plate and one small plate. Cut a notch for the mouth (a small triangle) in the other small plate. Glue the pieces together, as shown.

Ladybug

Use two plates, another small circle (maybe a muffin cup) and a pipe cleaner. Cut one plate in half. Bend the pipe cleaner in half and loop the ends. Glue it all together, as shown. Make sure to add the ladybug's spots! *(continued on next page)*

Turtle

Use two plates. Cut the rim of one plate into five pieces. Draw, color or cut them to look like feet and a tail. Color and cut out a head from the middle of the same plate. Add texture to the other plate to make it look like the turtle's shell. Glue it all together, as shown.

Piggy

Use one large plate, one small plate and construction paper scraps. Use the scraps to make the pig's feet, nose and ears. Cut a spiral, as shown, to make the curly tail. Color all the pieces pink or grey. Glue it all together, as shown.

Bunny Rabbit

Use one large plate and two small plates. Cut one small plate in half. Color everything pink and white. Glue together as shown. Add pipe cleaner whiskers and a cotton ball tail.

Elephant

Use one large plate and three small plates. Cut the rim off one large plate. Cut it in half to use as the trunk. Glue together, as shown. Add eyes, feet and tusks, if desired.

Suggestions

- Cut a tail, tusks, legs, ears, antennae, whiskers and other parts from paper plate rims; or use pipe cleaners, drinking straws or yarn stiffened with glue for texture.

- When dry, paint or color your animal, adding stripes, spots and other features. Paint on eyes or glue on plastic wiggly eyes.

- Attach picture mounts or glue yarn looped to the back of the plates to hang your animal.

- Try some of the other animals shown below.

Thumbprint Animals

These animals are original since you use your own fingerprints to make them! See how many different animals you can create!

Here's how . . .

1. Roll your fingertip or thumb over the stamp pad.

2. Press it onto the paper.

3. Add animal details (eyes, nose, whiskers, teeth, etc.) with the crayons.

What you'll need

- ☐ several stamp pads (black or purple work well)
- ☐ white paper
- ☐ crayons, colored pencils or markers

Suggestions

- Staple several sheets together at the top to form a notepad.

- Use your stamped paper to make greeting cards, book covers or wrapping paper.

- Write a story and illustrate it with these simple characters.

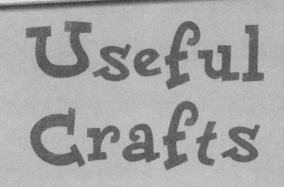

Useful Crafts

The Useful Crafts section features objects you can really use. And once you've decorated them, these crafts will be more than useful—they'll look great, too.

In this section, you will find a variety of interesting projects, from bird feeders to bulletin boards. Many of the crafts are items you will want to use every day, such as the Mirror Plate or the Piggy Bank. And other projects, such as the Treasure Box, are excellent choices to give as gifts.

Use the crafts as suggested, or make up your own uses for them. For example, you might use the Wind Sock to study weather patterns by watching the streamers for wind speed and direction. Be creative!

Pine Cone Bird Feeder

Fun to make and fun to watch, this natural bird feeder may become a favorite hangout for your feathered friends right outside your window!

What you'll need

- ☐ pine cone
- ☐ peanut butter
- ☐ birdseed or bread crumbs
- ☐ butter knife or spoon
- ☐ string

Here's how . . .

1. Tie the string around the pine cone.

2. Use the knife to spread peanut butter over the cone.

3. Roll the covered cone in birdseed or bread crumbs.

4. Hang the feeder outside near a window.

5. Watch to see who will eat from it.

Barrette Holder

You'll never wonder where your barrettes are after you make this fun Barrette Holder!

What you'll need

- two 9" paper plates
- crayons, felt-tip pens, watercolors, tempera or acrylic paints
- heavy rug yarn (about 1/2 skein)
- colored ribbons
- white glue
- yardstick
- scissors
- rubber bands

Here's how . . .

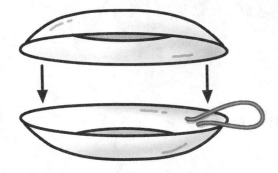

1. Loop a piece of yarn to be the hanger.

2. To make the head, glue the rims of the plates together with the eating sides facing each other, as shown. Glue the hanger between the two plates at the same time.

3. Color a face on one of the plates.

4. When dry, glue a few strands of yarn to the forehead to make bangs.

5. For braids, cut 18 strands of yarn, each 1 3/4 yards long.

6. About 5 inches from one end, secure the yarn with a rubber band.

7. Divide the yarn into three equal parts (6 strands each) and braid it. About 5 inches from the other end, secure it again with a rubber band.

8. To make two braids from the one long braid, tie a piece of yarn around the braid, midway from the ends.

9. Put glue on the rim of the face plate where the hair would be. Place the braids around the face.

10. Tie the ribbons over the rubber bands.

Suggestion

● Have an adult use hot glue to make it last longer.

Wind Sock

Make this Wind Sock out of your favorite colors! Hang it outside, or use it as a decoration for your room.

What you'll need

- [ ] old window shade
- [ ] yarn
- [ ] paper clip
- [ ] crayons, markers or paint
- [ ] glue or stapler
- [ ] scissors
- [ ] ruler
- [ ] paper hole punch
- [ ] crepe paper (optional)

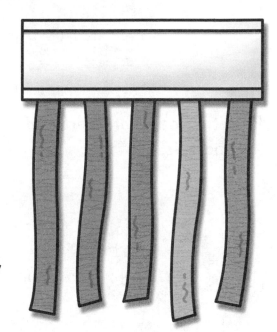

Here's how . . .

1. Cut the window shade to be 6 inches by 18 inches. This will be the top strip.

2. Color the top strip with bright bold shapes.

3. Cut five strips from the shade to be 3 inches by 18 inches, and glue them to the back of the top strip, as shown. Or use five strips of crepe paper.

4. Cut two strips of the shade to be 1/2 inch by 18 inches, and glue them over the top strip to make it more sturdy.

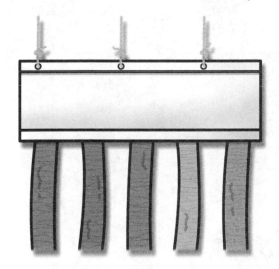

5. Use a ruler to place a dot at 1 inch, 7 inches and 13 inches from the left edge of the top strip.

6. Punch out the dots with a hole punch.

7. Thread a piece of yarn through each hole and tie a knot to secure each piece, as shown.

8. Glue the ends of the top strip together.

9. Gather the yarn ends and tie one large loop or knot.

10. Open a paper clip to make a hook for hanging the wind sock, as shown.

197

Bulletin Board

Bulletin boards are perfect for displaying your favorite photos, school papers and posters!

What you'll need

- ☐ foam board (or foam sheet)
- ☐ fabric
- ☐ tacks or stapler
- ☐ ribbon
- ☐ paper clip
- ☐ glue

List for sleepover:
- ✓ teddy bear
- ✓ pillow
- ✓ games

Josh and Sammie

Me

Here's how . . .

1. Cover the foam board with a piece of fabric large enough to cover the front and back.

2. Keep the fabric in place by using tacks to attach it on the back.

3. Glue the ribbon around the edge of the bulletin board for a border.

4. To make a hook, use a tack to fasten a large paper clip on the back.

Suggestion

● Decorate your board as much as you wish. You may want to add more to the border or your name to the board.

Piggy Bank

Saving money is fun when you can feed a happy pig in the process!

What you'll need

- ☐ 2 disposable soup bowls
- ☐ lightweight cardboard
- ☐ pipe cleaner
- ☐ 4 thread spools, film canisters or corks
- ☐ tempera or acrylic paints, or felt-tip pens
- ☐ paintbrushes
- ☐ white glue
- ☐ pencil
- ☐ scissors
- ☐ paper hole punch
- ☐ an adult

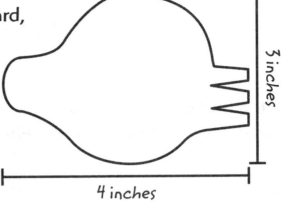

3 inches

4 inches

1. Make a drawing of the pig's head on cardboard, including the tabs, as shown. Then, cut it out.

2. Cut a 1 1/4 inch slit at the side of one bowl.

3. Slide the head into the slit and bend out the tabs and glue them to the inside of the bowl, as shown.

4. Punch a small hole in the bowl on the side opposite the head and insert a curled pipe cleaner as a tail. Glue or tape the pipe cleaner to the inside of the bowl to secure it.

5. Have an adult cut a slot in the center of the pig's back, large enough for a quarter to fall through (about 1/4 inch wide and 1 1/2 inches long).

6. To make the body, apply glue to the rim of the other bowl and put the bowl with the pig's head directly on it, as shown. Let them dry.

7. To make legs, glue four thread spools to the bottom of the pig. Let them dry.

8. Paint your pig, and add a snout and other features.

Butterfly Magnet

Here is one butterfly that won't fly away! Use this magnet to hold special papers and pictures on your refrigerator.

What you'll need

- ☐ miniature clothespin
- ☐ tissue paper
- ☐ adhesive magnetic tape
- ☐ pipe cleaners
- ☐ glue
- ☐ scissors

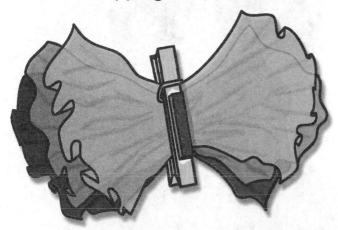

Here's how . . .

1. Cut three pieces of tissue paper into 3-inch squares.

2. Gather one square in the middle and clip the clothespin around it, as shown.

3. Repeat step 2 with the other two pieces of tissue paper, overlapping the pieces.

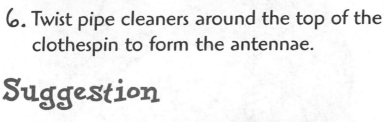

4. Put several drops of glue on the clothespin to hold the tissue paper in place. Be careful not to rip the tissue paper when you open the clothespin.

5. Cut a piece of magnetic tape to glue to the back of the butterfly, as shown.

6. Twist pipe cleaners around the top of the clothespin to form the antennae.

Suggestion

- Have an adult use hot glue to make it last longer.

Treasure Box

Design your own special box that opens and closes. Use it to hold your favorite treasures!

What you'll need

- [ ] 2 disposable soup bowls
- [ ] hairpin or twisty tie
- [ ] crayons, felt-tip pens, watercolors, tempera or acrylic paints
- [ ] white glue
- [ ] small round button or bead
- [ ] paper hole punch
- [ ] decorative stickers, glitter, ribbon, etc. (optional)

Here's how . . .

1. To make a hinged box, punch two holes about 1 inch apart through the rims of the two bowls.

2. Thread a hairpin through each pair of holes and twist the ends to make it secure, as shown.

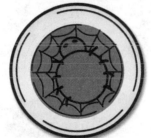
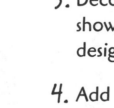

3. Decorate the box. Use an idea shown here or create your own design.

4. Add stickers or other decorations, if desired.

5. Glue the button to the front of the lid to make opening and closing easier.

Lid Pincushion

Make this pretty pincushion to hold your pins. Make an extra one to give as a gift!

What you'll need

- ☐ cotton
- ☐ lid from a peanut butter jar
- ☐ fabric
- ☐ ribbon or yarn
- ☐ pins and needles
- ☐ rubber band
- ☐ glue (optional)

Here's how . . .

1. Fill the lid with cotton.

2. Cover the lid and cotton with a circle of fabric.

3. Wrap the rubber band around the lid to secure the fabric. Cover the rubber band by gluing or tying the ribbon over it.

4. Stick your pins and needles into the cushion for safekeeping and easy finding.

Suggestion

● For another version of this idea, keep the jar as well. Cover the top of the lid with cotton, then follow steps 2–4. Fill the jar with decorative items, such as dried beans, seashells, buttons, etc. Then, screw the lid back onto the jar.

Plate Mirror

Every face needs a mirror. Use colored yarn to match your room!

What you'll need

- [ ] 1 sturdy 9" paper plate
- [ ] 1 round mirror, not more than 5 inches in diameter (across)
- [ ] yarn in different colors
- [ ] glue
- [ ] paper clip
- [ ] scissors
- [ ] toothpick
- [ ] pencil
- [ ] sponge

1. Glue the mirror to the center of the paper plate and let it dry.

2. Make a colorful border around the plate by gluing yarn to the rim. Use a toothpick to press and guide the yarn. Cut the yarn where the ends meet and press them together.

3. In the same way as step 2, glue yarn around the edge of the mirror, so that the mirror's edges are covered, as shown.

4. Draw bold, simple designs with a pencil, staying within the borders.

5. Outline the main design areas with yarn. *(continued on next page)*

6. Fill in the small areas, one at a time, by winding a single piece of yarn inward from the border to the center. Use a variety of colors to fill it in. Apply glue as you need it. Use a clean damp sponge to remove any extra glue. Continue doing this until the plate is completely covered with yarn.

7. When dry, attach a paper clip to the back of the plate for hanging, as shown.

Suggestion

● Have an adult use hot glue to make it last longer.

Holiday Projects

What would the holidays be without colorful decorations? Think of a plump Thanksgiving turkey, a ghoulish Halloween monster or a bright red Valentine's Day heart. The Holiday Projects section features projects for many major American holidays. And by changing colors here and shapes there, you can make many of these crafts for different celebrations.

For example, the Halloween Pumpkin Lantern can be changed to look like Abraham Lincoln or Father Time. And you can make the Father's Day Planter into a gift for a grandparent or a friend. Let your imagination go wild! And have a happy holiday, too.

Gift Wrapping Decorations

Make these decorations instead of a bow when wrapping a gift. Or make them into ornaments to hang!

What you'll need

- ☐ construction paper in different colors
- ☐ ribbon, yarn or string
- ☐ stapler
- ☐ glue or tape
- ☐ ruler
- ☐ scissors

1. Cut construction paper into 1 inch by 12 inch strips.

2. Arrange the strips in alternate colors. Then, staple the strips together in the middle, as shown.

3. Create various designs by folding and gluing or curling the top and bottom ends of the stapled strips.

4. Use ribbons to attach them to holiday presents.

Suggestions

● Use these as ornaments on your Christmas tree.

● Use red and green paper for Christmas; blue and white for Hanukkah; red, black and green for Kwanza.

● There are endless ways to fold the paper strips—use your imagination to make up your own.

Pop-Up Cards

Send a card with a fun surprise inside to make someone feel extra special!

What you'll need

- ☐ three or more sheets of 9" x 12" construction paper
- ☐ crayons or markers
- ☐ glue
- ☐ scissors
- ☐ ruler

Dear Mom,
I hope you have a nice Easter. I love you very much.
XXOOXO Sa...

BOO BASH

It's out of this world!

at Sally's house

Oct. 31
7:00 PM

Figure Pop-Up

1. Fold two sheets of construction paper in half, as shown.

2. Write or color a message or design for the front of the card with the open wide side on the bottom. This is the outside of your card.

3. On the blank folded paper, cut two 1 1/2-inch slits about 1 inch apart around the midpoint, as shown. Make sure the slits are the same length.

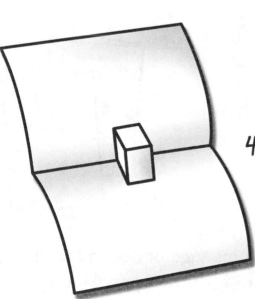

4. Unfold the paper and push the strip from the outside so that it folds into the card, as shown.

5. Color and cut out a figure up to 5 inches tall from the last sheet of construction paper. (continued on next page)

6. Glue the figure only to the front facing part of the inside strip. If the figure is taller than the strip, glue the bottom part just up to the fold of the strip.

7. On the inside of the paper, color a scene on the top half around the figure, and write a message on the bottom half. This is the inside of your card.

Dear Mom,
I hope you have a nice Easter. I love you very much!
XXOOXO Sam

8. Glue the outside sheet of the card to the inside sheet. Do *not* glue the strip with the figure but leave it folded the opposite way, as shown.

9. Send your card to a friend for a special day.

Munch Mouth Pop-Up

1. Fold two sheets of construction paper in half, as shown.

YOU'RE INVITED TO . . .

2. Write or color a message or design for the front of the card with the open wide side on the right. This is the outside of your card.

3. On the other sheet, put a dot on the center of the folded edge, as shown.

4. Draw a 2-inch line from the dot towards the middle of the card, as shown.

5. Cut on the line, beginning at the dot.

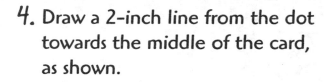

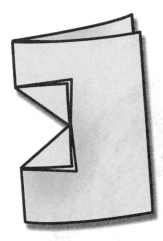

6. Fold back both flaps created to form two triangles, as shown.

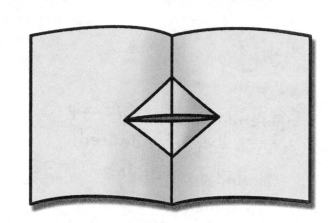

7. Open the flaps. Then, open the entire sheet of paper.

8. Turn over the paper so it looks like a tent. Put the finger of one hand on the top flap and push down. From the back (with your other hand, using your first finger and thumb) pinch the edges together.

9. Repeat step 8 with the bottom flap to form the mouth.

10. Draw a person or creature around the mouth.

11. Glue the inside and outside card parts together. Do not put glue near the area of the pop-up mouth!

Bubble Print Gift Wrap

For fun wrapping paper, make this wet and wild bubble project!

What you'll need

- tempera paint (1/2 cup of each color desired)
- liquid dishwashing detergent (1/2 cup for each color desired)
- straws (not flexible)
- construction, tissue or fingerpaint paper (11" x 18" or larger works best), or plain paper bags
- water
- quart-sized containers
- shallow pans
- apron or old clothes

Here's how . . .

1. For each color you want to use, make the following mixture the night before: 1/2 cup tempera paint and 1/2 cup liquid dishwashing detergent in a quart container. Add about 1/4 cup water, then stir. Let the mixtures set overnight, so they stay properly mixed. Wear the apron every time you work with the paint.

2. When you are ready to make the prints, pour each paint mixture into a shallow pan.

3. Place the paper on the pan over the mixture. Place one end of the straw under the paper, into the mixture.

4. Blow through the straw to make bubbles in the mixture. (Only blow through the straw—be sure not to suck in!) When the bubbles break, they will make a design on the paper.

5. Try several colors on the same paper.

6. When dried, wrap presents with your paper.

Suggestion

● Blow bubbles onto the paper with different types of bubble wands to make your prints. This way is much messier but very fun to watch. Consider wearing goggles for this!

Fuzzy Valentine

This cuddly bear makes a great Valentine card to send a hug to someone special.

What you'll need

- [ ] brown and red construction paper
- [ ] brown and red yarn
- [ ] cardboard
- [ ] newspaper
- [ ] pencil
- [ ] scissors
- [ ] glue
- [ ] tempera paint
- [ ] construction paper scraps
- [ ] old paintbrush (optional)
- [ ] toothpick (optional)

Here's how . . .

1. Cover your working surface with newspaper.

2. Cut out a bear shape from the brown construction paper.

3. Glue the bear shape to the cardboard and cut it out.

4. Cut brown yarn pieces about 1/2 inch long.

5. Pull apart the strands of yarn, as shown.

6. With your finger or a brush, spread glue onto the bear's body and press the yarn into the glue. If desired, use a toothpick to press and guide the yarn. Do a small area at a time until the bear is covered.

7. Tie the red yarn around the bear's neck.

8. Cut out a large red heart and glue the bear on top of the heart.

9. Paint a message to your Valentine. Add a face with construction paper and yarn.

Patterned Shamrocks

Good luck will be with you when you cut and decorate these shamrocks on Saint Patrick's Day!

What you'll need

- [ ] cardboard
- [ ] drawing paper
- [ ] crayons or markers in shades of green
- [ ] pencil

Here's how . . .

1. Make at least two copies of the shamrock patterns below on cardboard and cut them out.

pattern

pattern

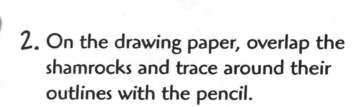

2. On the drawing paper, overlap the shamrocks and trace around their outlines with the pencil.

3. Color different designs within each shamrock.

Paper Maché Easter Egg

Everyone will want to know how you made this magical egg. It looks even better hanging in the sun!

What you'll need

- assorted colors of tissue paper
- balloon (round, not long)
- 1/2 cup flour
- salt (so the maché doesn't mold)
- 1 cup warm water
- paper clip
- yarn
- baking pan
- newspaper
- apron or old clothes
- pin, paper clip or anything sharp to break the balloon

1. Cover your working surface with newspaper and wear an apron over your clothes.

2. Blow up the balloon part of the way and tie a knot in the end. Stick a paper clip through the knot.

3. Tear the tissue paper into strips or squares.

4. Combine flour, water and salt in the baking pan. Mix it with your hands until it has a soupy consistency.

5. Dip a tissue paper strip into the mixture. Then, wrap it around the balloon.

6. Continue dipping and wrapping tissue paper, overlapping each one, until you have covered the balloon except for a hole the size of a quarter around the balloon's knot. You may want to add several layers around the balloon.

7. Let the balloon dry. This may take overnight to do.

8. Pop the balloon with the pin and pull it out using the paper clip in the knot.

9. Use the paper clip stuck through the opening and a piece of yarn or string to hang it. Hang your egg design from the ceiling or outside on an "Easter tree."

Eggshell Mosaic

Mosaics are pictures made up of small things like tiles or glass. Try this mosaic using dyed eggshells.

What you'll need

- dyed eggshells from Easter eggs
- poster board
- markers
- newspaper
- glue
- pencil

1. Cover your working surface with newspaper.

2. Crush the colored eggshells into small, but not tiny, pieces.

3. Using a pencil, draw a simple shape on a piece of poster board.

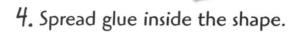

4. Spread glue inside the shape.

5. Sprinkle eggshells onto your glue shape. Let it dry, then shake off the extra shell pieces.

6. Color a background, if desired.

Suggestions

- Instead of sprinkling the shells, arrange them by color on your design.

- Use white eggshells instead of colored ones. Use watercolors to lightly paint the shells *after* you have completed your design.

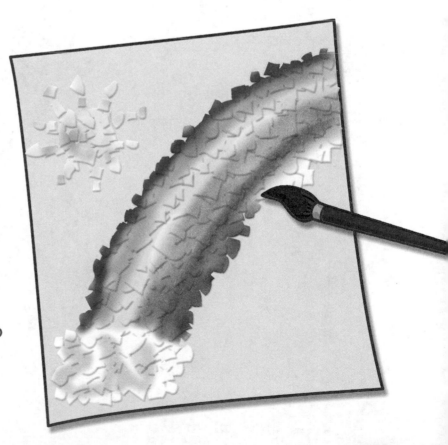

May Basket

Continue this fun tradition! Make this pretty basket, fill it with flowers or candies and hang it on someone's doorknob on May Day.

What you'll need

- ☐ two 9" paper plates
- ☐ paints, crayons or felt-tip pens
- ☐ plastic lid from a 1-lb. coffee can
- ☐ paper hole punch
- ☐ 1 yard narrow ribbon or yarn
- ☐ circle stencil about 3" in diameter
- ☐ ruler
- ☐ pencil
- ☐ white glue
- ☐ scissors
- ☐ plastic wrap (optional)
- ☐ flowers, candy or another treat (optional)
- ☐ stapler (optional)

1. Paint the front and back of one paper plate. Let it dry.

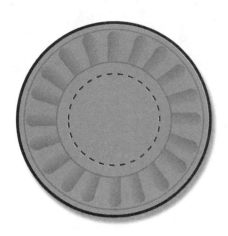

2. Use the stencil to lightly trace a circle in the center of the painted plate. This will be the bottom of the basket.

3. On the inner circle you just drew, lay out nine points equally spaced around the circle. Then, lightly draw lines from the center of the circle through the points to the outside edge of the plate, as shown. You may want an adult to help you with this step.

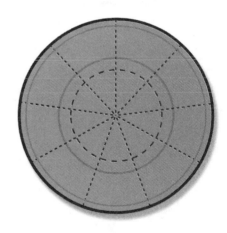

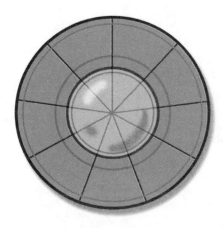

4. Use the stencil to trace a circle onto the plastic lid.

5. Cut out and glue the plastic circle over the drawn circle on the plate, as shown. Let it dry.

(continued on next page)

6. Cut along the penciled lines from the outer edge of the plate to the inner plastic circle forming wedge-shaped sections.

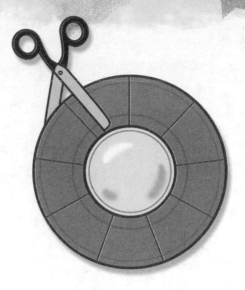

7. Trim the top of each section into a rounded petal shape.

8. Punch two holes in each "petal" about 1/2 inch apart and 1 1/3 inches up from the bottom of the basket.

9. Gently bend each "petal" up and crease each one around the plastic circle, as shown.

10. Weave the ribbon through the holes in the petals and tie them into a bow.

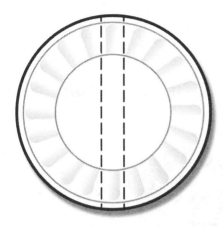

11. For a handle, cut a 3/4 inch by 9 inch strip from the other plate.

12. Paint the handle. When dry, glue or staple the handle to the inside edge of the basket.

13. Line your basket with plastic wrap first if you add candy or flowers.

Mother's Day BoxCard

Mom will get a real surprise when she opens this box. It's a BoxCard!

What you'll need

- [ ] 9" × 12" light construction paper
- [ ] white construction paper
- [ ] crayons or markers
- [ ] scissors
- [ ] tape or glue

Here's how . . .

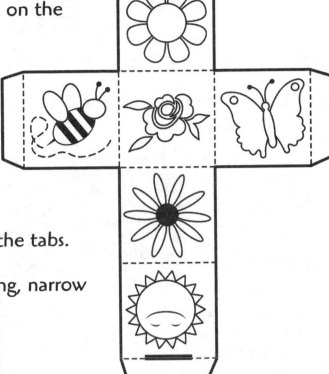

1. Make a larger copy of the box pattern on the right on light construction paper.

2. Cut out the box pattern along the outer solid lines.

3. Color the sides.

4. Fold in on all small dotted lines.

5. Tape the sides of the box together at the tabs.

6. Write a Mother's Day message on a long, narrow strip of the white paper.

7. Fold the strip like a fan, as shown.

8. Tape the end of the strip on the inside of the box.

9. Cut a slit in the top and close the box.

Suggestion

- Use this as a card for any holiday, including Father's Day or Grandparents' Day.

Father's Day Planter

Give Dad some grass he doesn't have to mow for Father's Day. Remember to start this in May!

What you'll need

- ☐ white foam drinking cup, large size
- ☐ potting soil
- ☐ rye grass seed
- ☐ 9" x 12" white construction paper
- ☐ crayons or markers
- ☐ scissors
- ☐ glue

Here's how . . .

1. Fill the cup 2/3 full with potting soil.

2. Sprinkle grass seed on top of the soil, then cover it with a thin layer of potting soil, as shown, and water.

3. Put the cup in a sunny place and water it every few days. It will take about 7 days for the grass to begin to grow and form the "hair" on the Father's Day Planter. Start the project 2–3 weeks before Father's Day to allow enough time for the grass to grow.

4. The day before you give this planter as a gift, color and cut out face parts from construction paper. Add features to make it look like your father!

5. Glue the face parts to the outside of the foam cup.

6. Be careful to keep it upright if you wrap this gift. A fancy gift bag would work best.

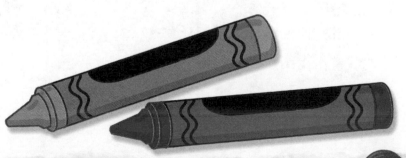

Fourth of July Fireworks

Make your own fireworks using paint, a straw, salt and a little hot air!

What you'll need

- [ ] 12" x 18" black construction paper
- [ ] light red, white and light blue tempera paint
- [ ] water
- [ ] salt
- [ ] plastic drinking straw
- [ ] paint dishes
- [ ] spoon

1. Thin some tempera with water to make it runny.

2. Use a spoon to place drops of the paint on the paper.

3. Hold the straw tilted and slightly above the paint. Blow from different directions to move the paint to create a starburst design. (Remember to always blow out—not suck in—through your straw when creating these paintings. The paint is great but not great tasting!)

4. Choose a different color and repeat the same procedure on another part of the paper. Designs can overlap.

5. Do the same thing using the third color.

6. While your painting is still wet, sprinkle it with salt. Gently shake off the extra salt after everything is dry.

paint

paint

Halloween Lantern

You can make this Halloween Lantern, or change the designs and hang it up for any holiday or party!

What you'll need

- ☐ 9" x 12" orange construction paper
- ☐ black construction paper
- ☐ scissors
- ☐ glue
- ☐ tape or stapler
- ☐ string or yarn
- ☐ ruler
- ☐ pencil
- ☐ paper hole punch
- ☐ orange and black crepe paper streamers (optional)

Here's how . . .

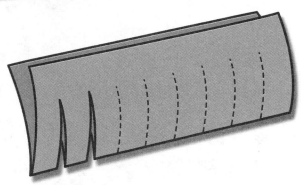

1. Fold the orange construction paper in half.

2. With a ruler, draw lines from the fold every inch, as shown. Stop 2 inches from the top.

3. Cut on the lines you have drawn.

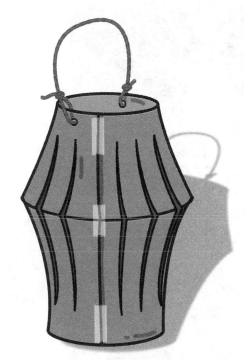

4. Unfold the paper and tape the ends of the lantern together.

5. Cut out the eyes, nose and mouth for the pumpkin from black construction paper, then glue them to the lantern.

6. Glue on crepe paper streamers, if desired.

7. To hang your lantern, punch holes in the top and hang it with a string, as shown.

Suggestions

- Make a black lantern cat using black construction paper for the body. Add eyes, ears, nose, mouth and whiskers.

- If you use crepe paper, make sure it doesn't get wet in the rain. The color will run.

Standing Monster

Look, it's Frankenstein! Use this project to make a mummy, Count Dracula or a group of ghosts!

What you'll need

- ☐ 2 brown paper lunch bags
- ☐ newspaper
- ☐ string or yarn
- ☐ paint, markers or crayons
- ☐ scissors
- ☐ glue
- ☐ tape
- ☐ decorative items, such as fabric, tissue paper, construction paper, buttons, rickrack, craft fur, etc. (optional)

Here's how . . .

1. Fill the lunch bags with loosely crumpled newspaper.

2. Fit one bag over the other. Tie it loosely one–third of the way down using string, as shown.

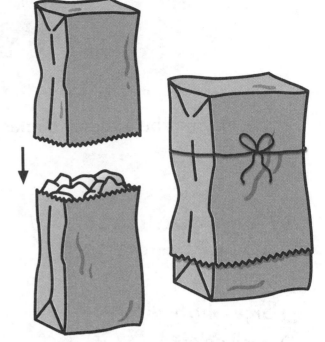

3. Use materials to create the face, hair, clothes, even arms and feet for your monster.

Sweet Turkey

He may not be a turkey dinner exactly, but this turkey is still delicious.

What you'll need

- ☐ apple
- ☐ large marshmallow
- ☐ small colored marshmallows or gum drops
- ☐ 2 cloves or raisins
- ☐ toothpicks
- ☐ vegetable peeler
- ☐ carrot
- ☐ ice water
- ☐ an adult

Here's how . . .

1. Have an adult help you use the peeler to cut thin carrot strips. Put them in a glass of ice water. They will curl themselves after a few minutes. These will be side wings and the wattle.

2. Attach the large marshmallow to the apple with a toothpick to form the head.

3. Push the cloves into the head to form the eyes.

4. Attach the small marshmallows to the body with toothpicks to form the feathers, as shown.

5. Attach the side wings and wattle (curled carrot strips) to the body with toothpicks.

Turkey Feathers

The whole family may want to give you a "hand" when making this great Thanksgiving decoration!

What you'll need

- ☐ colorful fall leaves, not too dry
- ☐ brown or orange butcher paper
- ☐ scissors
- ☐ glue or stapler
- ☐ pencil
- ☐ crayons, markers or paint

Here's how . . .

1. Draw a large turkey shape on the butcher paper, as shown.

2. Cut out the turkey shape.

3. Glue leaves onto the turkey to form the tail feathers, as shown.

4. Color other features on your turkey.

Suggestion

● Instead of using leaves, trace your own hand onto construction paper. Add a short phrase about something for which you are thankful. Do this several times and get hand shapes from other family members' hands. Cut out the hands and glue them to the turkey body.

my family

my dog

my food

my house

my health

my bike

my friends

my clothes

my guinea pig

I am thankful for . . .

245

Paint-Spray Designs

You can use your favorite cookie cutters to make designs for this really cool paint-spray project.

What you'll need

- ☐ holiday shape patterns (cookie cutters work well)
- ☐ cardboard
- ☐ construction paper in dark colors
- ☐ white tempera paint
- ☐ old toothbrush
- ☐ craft stick
- ☐ pie pan
- ☐ pins
- ☐ newspaper
- ☐ scissors

Here's how . . .

1. Make patterns from the holiday shapes on cardboard and cut them out.

2. Cover your working surface with newspaper.

3. Pin the cardboard patterns in a design on construction paper.

4. Pour a small amount of white paint into the pie pan.

5. Dip the toothbrush in the paint and hold it facedown over your design.

6. Rub the craft stick under the toothbrush, rubbing away from your face.

7. After the paint dries, remove the pins and patterns.

8. Add a construction paper frame.

Suggestion

● You could paint these on a wide ribbon and hang it around your Christmas tree.

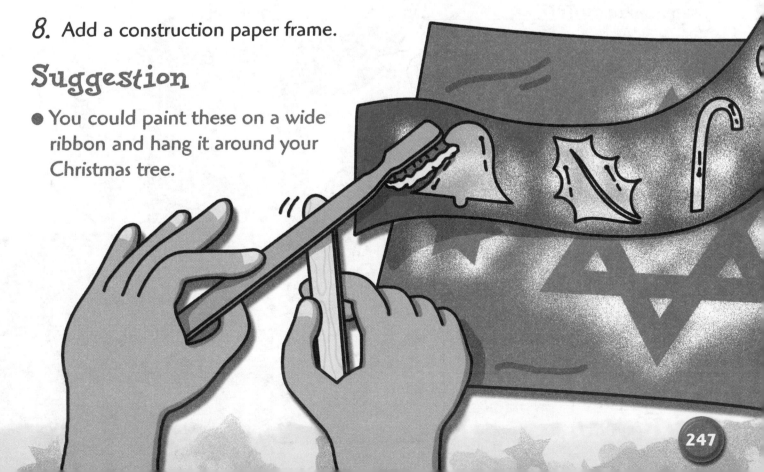

Cookie Cutter Ornaments

These ornaments will be popular gifts—and they're lots of fun to make! They are perfect to add when gift-wrapping, instead of a bow.

What you'll need

- [ ] 2 cups flour
- [ ] 1 cup salt
- [ ] 2/3 cup water
- [ ] felt-tip pens
- [ ] cookie cutters
- [ ] glue
- [ ] ribbon
- [ ] paper clips
- [ ] photographs of you
- [ ] mixing bowl
- [ ] round cutting tool smaller than your picture
- [ ] wax paper (optional)
- [ ] rolling pin (optional)
- [ ] clear plastic spray, available in art supply stores (optional)
- [ ] an adult

Here's how . . .

1. The night before you do this project, make the following recipe in the mixing bowl: Mix the dry ingredients with your hands, then add water. Add more water as needed to create a mixture the texture of stiff pie dough.

2. The next day, roll out the dough with a rolling pin or pat it out to about 1/4 inch thick.

3. Cut out the dough with cookie cutters. Using the round cutting tool, cut a hole in the center of each shape.

4. Push a paper clip through the top of each shape for the hook.

5. Let the shapes dry out for several days. It is best to keep them on wax paper.

6. When the shapes are dry, decorate them with felt-tip pens.

7. Have an adult help you spray the shapes with clear plastic spray, if desired.

8. Carefully place glue around the edges of the hole on the back of each shape.

9. Glue your photograph on the back of each shape. If the hole is larger than the photograph, glue your picture onto a piece of round paper, then glue the paper to the back of the shape.

10. Tie a ribbon around the paper clip to hang each ornament.

Pasta Ornaments

Use different shapes and sizes of pasta to make interesting textures for your ornaments. Get your friends together and have a pasta decoration party!

What you'll need

- ☐ pasta noodles of all shapes
- ☐ construction paper in holiday colors
- ☐ yarn
- ☐ glue
- ☐ scissors
- ☐ paper hole punch

Here's how . . .

1. Cut the construction paper into a circle about the size of a cookie. Punch a hole near the edge of the circle and tie a loop of yarn through the hole for hanging.

2. Using different pasta shapes, make an attractive arrangement on the construction paper.

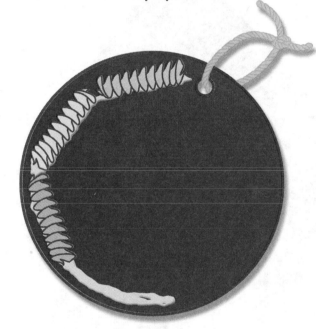

3. Glue each piece onto your circle.

4. Let it dry, then hang it up.

Suggestions

- Dry cereal, beans, shells, etc. would also make nice textured ornaments.

- Try using a toothpick to move a noodle into place or to glue it.

- Have an adult use hot glue to make it last longer.

Face Mobile

The lightest breeze will bring your character to life!
It's fun to make and fun to watch!

What you'll need

- [ ] two 9" paper plates
- [ ] scissors
- [ ] construction paper
- [ ] white thread
- [ ] white glue
- [ ] paper hole punch
- [ ] gummed loose-leaf reinforcement
- [ ] plastic curtain ring
- [ ] fiberfill, yarn, cotton, craft fur or curled gift ribbon for hair

Here's how . . .

1. Carefully cut the centers from the paper plates so that the rims remain together, as shown.

2. Decide who or what your character is going to be. Cut ears, eyes, eyebrows, a nose, a mouth, cheeks, a hat, a tie, a mustache or whatever you need for your character from construction paper. Make enough for 2 faces.

3. Position the construction paper parts inside one of the plate rims. Be sure the pieces are well-spaced so that your mobile will turn freely.

4. Measuring from the rim, cut lengths of thread long enough to join the parts.

5. Glue each set of parts together, sandwiching the thread between them. This is needed so each feature will be the same on both sides as it turns.

(continued on next page)

6. Put a small amount of glue around the outside of one rim. Place the other rim on top, matching the edges of both plates, as shown. Let it dry.

7. Glue hair and other features to your character.

8. Punch a hole at the top center of the hat. Put a gummed reinforcement around the hole.

9. Tie a long thread from the hole to the curtain ring to make hanging your mobile easier.

Suggestions

- Have an adult use hot glue to make it last longer.

- Try your own characters.

Index

● supplies from home
● especially quick and easy
● needs adult supervision